Semiotics
and
Church Architecture

To my colleague
Mark Searle
(September 19, 1941-August 16, 1992)

I have lived the paschal mystery long enough not to
foresake it or to doubt it just when it becomes most
real

The quote above was taken from a letter Mark Searle wrote me on
Thanksgiving Day 1991

Liturgia condenda is published by the liturgical Institute of the
Theological Department of Tilburg (NL). The series plans to publish
innovative research into the science of liturgy and serve as a forum which
will bring together publications produced by researchers of various natio-
nalities. The motto *liturgia condenda* expresses the conviction that
research into the various aspects of liturgy can make a critico-normative
contribution to the deepening and the renewal of liturgical practice.
The editorial board: Lambert Leyssen (Louvain), Gerard Lukken (Tilburg), Gerard Rouwhorst (Utrecht), Anton Scheer (Nijmegen), Louis van
Tongeren (Tilburg), and Charles Caspers (secretary – Tilburg).

Semiotics
and
Church Architecture

**Applying the Semiotics of A.J.Greimas
and the Paris School to the analysis
of church buildings**

Gerard Lukken and Mark Searle

Kok Pharos Publishing House

CIP-GEGEVENS KONINKLIJKE BIBLIOTHEEK, DEN HAAG

© 1993, Kok Pharos Publishing House.
P.O. Box 130, 8260 AC Kampen, The Netherlands
Photos by Robin Cohen
Cover Design by Dik Hendriks
ISBN 90 390 0063 8
NUGI 636
Typesetting: Elgraphic bv, Schiedam

Contents

Preface

In recent decades, semiotics has succeeded in establishing itself as a discipline with international recognition. As a discipline specifically devoted to the study of signs and sign-systems, it is of course relevant to any number of other disciplines which in one way or another are involved with signs, whether linguistic or non-linguistic. Theology is one example, working as it constantly does with both verbal and non-verbal signs. Despite a good deal of resistance, semiotics has begun to establish itself in various theological disciplines, and here the kind of semiotics developed by A.J. Greimas and the so-called Paris School has proved particularly suitable for analyzing the different forms in which the Christian faith has found expression. It has been used extensively in biblical studies, for example, thanks particularly to the pioneering work of the Lyons-based group, CADIR (*Centre pour l'Analyse du Discours Religieux*). Since 1976, a Dutch study group, drawing on members of the Tilburg Theological Faculty and the Catholic Theological University at Utrecht, and operating under the name of SEMANET (*Semiotische Analyse door Nederlandse Theologen*), has been similarly engaged in applying Greimassian semiotics to various expressions of Christian faith, including biblical texts. But what distinguishes the Dutch group is the fact that its members represent several theological disciplines: biblical studies, catechetics, and liturgical studies.

The presence of liturgical studies in this group has led to interest gradually being taken in applying semiotics to non-linguistic expressions of faith. After all, liturgy is a syncretic phenomenon, employing a wide range of codes or, better, manifestation-languages. (Manifestation, as opposed to immanence, refers to the realization of significant form in a given substance; for example, musical sounds, gesture, spatial arrangements, iconography, and so on.) Now the great advantage of Greimas's semiotics is that it offers a single homogeneous metalanguage capable of being applied to all these different manifestations, thereby enabling us to study them in an integrated way. So, after an initial period in which the focus was on texts, SEMANET has more recently moved to the analysis of non-linguistic sign-systems, and it was at this stage that my colleague, Mark Searle of the University of Notre Dame (Indiana, U.S.A.) joined our working group. His contribution was to take the analytical method which I had worked out on the basis of semiotic theory and apply it to an actual church, that of SS. Peter and Paul in Tilburg, which is of interest both as a representative modern church building and as particularly intriguing object for semiotic analysis. This book, then, represents the fruits of our semiotic research. It shows how Greimassian semiotic theory as it relates to architecture was developed into a usable method for analyzing actual buildings and then demonstrates how such an analysis might be conducted.

The metalanguage of the Paris School is, of course, rather complicated. It borrows a number of terms from linguistics and invests them with rather specific meanings, as well as creating neologisms of its own. Obviously, it is not possible to provide, within the parameters of this book, a complete account of this metalanguage, which is in any case in continuing process of development. A comprehensive summary of Greimassian semiotics can be found in J. Courtés, *Analyse sémiotique du discours. De l'énoncé à l'énonciation*, Paris 1991, and in part one of the SEMANET publication, *Semiotiek en christelijke uitingsvormen*, Hilversum 1987, 9-54. For a fuller account, we refer the reader to the writings of A.J. Greimas, and especially to the two-volume *Sémiotique. Dictionnaire raisonné de la théorie du langage*, Paris 1979, 1986 (English translation of vol.1, *Semiotics and Language. An Analytical Dictionary*, Bloomington, IN 1982). Ongoing research by the Parish School is published in *Actes Sémiotiques* (since 1989 *Nouveaux Actes Sémiotiques*).

The book falls into two parts. The first deals with semiotic theory. Chapter One offers a general overview of space and architecture from the standpoint of Greimassian semiotics. Chapter Two then shows how Greimas's metalanguage can be used for the analysis of architecture, while Chapter Three develops a more specific architectural semiotic for use with church buildings. In the second part, theory yields to practice with a detailed analysis of the church of SS. Peter and Paul in Tilburg, using the methodology presented earlier. Chapter Four begins with the exterior of the church, while Chapter Five follows with an analysis of the interior. Bibliography, index, and appendices are provided at the end.

Shortly after the manuscript was completed, Mark Searle, aged 51, died of an incurable disease. May this book be a posthumous tribute to him as an exceptionally amiable colleague and a competent and creative liturgical scholar.

Our thanks are due to Thijs Michels who helped with the English translation and who, with Willem Marie Speelman, reviewed and edited the typescript. We also wish to acknowledge with gratitude the support received for this research from the 'Theologische Faculteit Tilburg' and the 'Mr. Paul De Gruyter Stichting'.

Gerard Lukken

Part I

Theory
by
Gerard Lukken

CHAPTER 1
Semiotics of Architecture

The semiotics of architecture may be regarded as one branch of a more broadly conceived semiotics of space (spatial semiotics). For this reason, it may be as well to begin by giving some general idea of what is involved in the semiotics of space before we turn more explicitly to a semiotics of architecture.

1. SEMIOTICS OF SPACE

According to Greimas, the starting point for a semiotics of space is extensiveness as such (Greimas/Courtés 1979: s.v. Espace, par. 1). Extensiveness, or area, refers to space as a continuous and undifferentiated dimension of reality. As such it is distinguished from what we will call 'place' which is a (human) construct, an object characterized by discontinuity or differentiation. When we talk of extensiveness as 'place', we introduce the things which occupy it and which introduce discontinuities into it. Extensiveness as our senses know it is not, in fact, continuous and undifferentiated. Instead, our senses perceive it as transformed and broken down into parts, so that one object is divided off from another as occupying its own space (Greimas/Courtés 1979: s.v. Espace, par. 1); Greimas 1976 (a): 129. In this way, indefinite 'area' is structured as a series of places, such as sea, land, city, village, woodland, field, pasture, road, buildings, interior rooms, and so forth.

In a way, subdividing 'area' into places like this represents a certain impoverishment of the real, lived experience of extensiveness. But this loss is compensated for by the gain in purposive signification (Greimas 1976 (a): 129), for the reconstruction of area as a series of places implies the construction of an actual semiotic object with space as its signifier.

Now 'space' is a broad term, capable of a number of different applications. We have already given some examples – sea, land, woodland and pasture, etc. – but the same term can also apply to a plan or map, to a scale model, a drawing, a painting, a photograph, a picture, or a sculpture. The term 'space' can also be used metaphorically. Here we are using 'space' in a narrower sense, but even so it encompasses several perspectives. It can be looked at from a strictly geometrical viewpoint, which considers it simply in terms of its being something quantifiable. But it is also possible to look at space more broadly as a matter of socio-cultural organization (i.e. as 'place'). From this angle, buildings are not only objects capable of measurement, but are seen as social and cultural entities. They serve to distance us from 'raw' nature and people are able to use them to express their social relationships. Consequently, people of different countries arrange their spaces very differently, as they demarcate their boundaries and organize their space within those boundaries in very different ways. The way space is organized in Belgium, for example, is quite different from that of the Netherlands, reflecting corresponding differences in social and cultural life. Given that a nation's identity is constructed, in part at least, in spatial terms, it is hardly surprising that the question is now constantly being raised in Europe of how national identities will be preserved once frontiers are done away with and barriers lifted to create a new and different 'place', namely that of a united Europe.

Greimassian semiotics prefers to look at space in such socio-cultural terms, seeing it as an 'utterance' (énoncé) constructed by a human subject to be read and utilized accordingly by a human subject. The space of the landscape, the city, the village or the house in which we live from day to day is already pre-shaped by others, and usually by a great many others. And this arrangement of human space is either affirmed and maintained or else it is altered when we in our turn come to use it. In our very use of it, a place as 'human utterance' is uttered anew and thus reconstituted either in its original meaning or in the new meaning that the user thereby confers on it. Thus the user-occupant is never purely passive: the very interaction with the space is a form of activity which constantly brings that space back into operation as a signifying utterance, so that it may or may not remain the same 'place' (Zilberberg 1984: 48).

Introducing the human subject into the definition of space in this way makes it necessary to take account, when reflecting on space, of all the ways in which that space may impinge upon the subject's sensorium. In other words, space needs to be considered not only in visual terms, but also in terms of its tactile, thermic, acoustic and aromatic qualities (Greimas/Courtés 1979: s.v Espace, par.2).

2. SEMIOTICS OF ARCHITECTURE

In recent decades, discussions on architecture and architectural theory have moved back and forth between three positions (Renier 1982: 10ff.).

First, in the 1950s, there were those who argued that architectural theory needed to be grounded in broad interdisciplinary cooperation. This provoked a reaction in the seventies, as theorists returned to championing the independence of architecture as a discipline. This was a reaction marked by renewed interest in the history of architecture. A third position is that occupied by the semiotics of architecture. For the Paris School, this began to develop in the early seventies when, in 1972, a conference was held in Paris on the semiotics of space, at which architecture also came up for discussion.

The term 'architecture' can be understood in a broad sense as applying to such things as gardens, landscapes, towns, villages, and so on; but in the Paris School it is used in the narrower sense as referring specifically to buildings. What is at issue here, then, is a specific kind of spatial semiotics. This semiotic perspective has the advantage of bringing together the strengths of both the other positions, for on the one hand it recognizes the autonomy of architecture as a discipline, while at the same time sharing the conviction that architecture as a sign-system cannot exist totally independently of other forms of semiotics. It is a matter of interdependence. This is the approach to a semiotics of architecture which will be followed in this book.

The semiotics of architecture, as developed by the Paris School, sees a building first of all as a single autonomous object and is concerned with its specific system of manifestation (i.e. how its meaning takes form in the data that confront our senses). It is important to understand what is meant by this. Architecture is the result of two processes: first there is the process whereby the building comes into existence, and second there is the process whereby the meaning of the building is altered by the many uses to which it is put in day-to-day living. Just as in spatial semiotics in general, so in architectural semiotics the subject is to be seen as integral to the production of meaning. The signification of a building, then, is produced by certain human subjects, only to be confirmed, modified or altered by those subsequently occupying it. Whether in the role of designer/builder or in the role of user/occupant, the consumer who assigns meaning to the building, the subject cannot be left out of the semiotics of architecture (Renier 1982:11). For this reason, architectural semiotics is never just concerned with the building as it comes from the hands of the builders, since those who use it are at least co-producers of its signification. It can well happen, for example, that the users or occupants redefine the building, altering its original meaning. They may come to enter with their guests through the back door rather than the front door, so that the main entrance no longer functions as such and the approach to the house is altered correspondingly. Especially in our days, when properties change hands so often even within a single generation and great store is set on adapting the building to the new occupant, it is important to realize that the way a building is actually used is part of the building's semiotic system. Thus architecture may be rightly characterized as an *oeuvre incessante*.

Yet architecture is not totally autonomous. It is connected to, and dependent upon, other branches of semiotics, and it is in that sense a syncretic object. Architecture only comes into existence through a whole series of mediating operations, none of which can be considered apart from the end product, the completed work. These mediating operations have to do with the concepts and uses governing the design of the building itself, with the fitting-out of the building for occupancy, and with the building itself as a place where certain social transactions take place. These mediating operations include many consultations, oral or written; technical, political or educational statements about the project; and even literary, scientific, legal or technical discourses.

Renier distinguishes the following semiotic items which may be involved in the creation of a new piece of architecture (Renier 1982: 12-13):

1)   Figurative (literary) discourses such as
      – architectural criticism (journals, newspaper articles)
      – announcements
      – presentations to the contractors and clients
      – presentations at exhibitions.

2) Non-figurative (legal and technical) discourses
      – specifications (description of the project, including information on design features, costs, etc.)
      – reports on the progress of the project
      – texts describing the project
      – technical reports on construction and outfitting
      – instructions relating to use of the building
      – regulations, norms, and technical directives.

3) Non-verbal texts
   a) projections:
      – plans and schemas such as organizational charts, flow charts, electrical grids, etc.
      – blueprints and construction plans
      – architectural drawings with or without perspective
      – scale models.

   b) construction and utilization of the building:
      – procedures for envisaging, constructing, outfitting and using the building

- presentation of the signification through the (inter)play of signifiers impinging on the senses of sight, hearing, smell and touch;
signifiers which are tied up with the building's design and
which relate to the perceived environment, social, physical and
climatic.

Referring to environmental phenomena such as those just mentioned,
Renier elsewhere coins the technical term 'biome' (Greimas/Courtés
1986: s.v. Biomatique (sémiotique -), Biome). The import of this term is
to indicate that the role of the architect is not just to outline a three-
dimensional body, but to take into account the facilities which will transform this 'space' into a 'place' where human beings can live and work.
Such facilities include controls to regulate temperature, lighting, and
noise within levels appropriate for the kind of building it is. Naturally,
the olfactory dimension (smell factor) may also be relevant. In these
ways, the natural site is transformed into an artificial setting which is no
longer at the mercy of nature's elements. Instead, the building offers
protection against immediate contact with the natural milieu, and thus
becomes what is technically designated a 'biome'. In French there is a play
on words as *lieu* is transformed into *milieu* ("*un milieu plus qu'un lieu*,"
Renier 1982: 13). So 'biome' means an environment created for human
living. It therefore consists of far more than just geometric categories
(topology, projective geometry, metrics) which merely refer to the
dimensions of that three-dimensional 'body' surrounding the place where
social living occurs. Rather 'biome' refers to the space insofar as it is
recognizable by its physical characteristics, such as those that give the
place its specific qualities of air, light, colour, sound, smell, and temperature.

Corresponding to the building as 'biome', there is a *sémiotique biomatique*, or semiotics of the biome which analyzes how architecture controls
the natural environment and creates artificial environments (Renier, in
Greimas/Courtés 1986: s.v. Biomatique (sémiotique -)). What it mainly
studies is enclosed space (*lieu englobé*) and the quality of air, temperature, light, sound and odour, qualities of some importance to those who
live and work there. As Renier points out, the original 'biome' consisted
of nothing more than a cave or a tent, which acted as a kind of membrane
to protect inhabitants against atmospheric conditions. What was important was the *englobé*, the space enclosed within the cave or the tent, not
the *englobant* which enclosed it. But, says Renier, this changed with the
construction of temples, when attention began to be paid to the membrane itself, bringing with it a move to the monumental. With that,
architecture was born. In recent times, however, there has come about a
re-thinking of the role of architecture. One indication of this is the preoc-

cupation with low-cost housing, the result of factors both economic and cultural. In a certain sense, this is like a return to origins in that the major preoccupation is with the inside (*englobé*) and not with the outside (*englobant*). Contemporary architecture hardly shares the monumental concerns of our ancestors. In our age, buildings are conceived from the inside out, with priority given to the functions, fittings and furnishings which will create an environment suitable for living.

There are other ways, too, in which architectural semiotics finds itself in a necessary relationship of interdependence with other areas of semiotics (Renier 1982: 13 ff.). These include:

- proxemics, or the semiotics of the body in relationship to its surrounding space, and of movement and gesture in space;
- semiotics of space conceived as a social environment filled with sounds, odours, and colours, as well as with people and objects present;
- semiotics of decor: here one thinks especially of the finishings or wall-hangings that circumscribe the space and the coverings that clothe the bodies occupying the space and that in turn contrast with the more permanent decor;
- semiotics of objects occupying the space, of the space they take up, and the gestures associated with them: furniture, ornaments, sculpture, paintings, and so forth. Such things help to mark and differentiate the space, while at the same time becoming, with the fixed decor, part of the environment of the space itself;
- semiotics of lighting: this includes the radical transformation ('renewed destruction') which lighting is capable of creating in the materials used in the space, in the appearance of their surfaces, and in the configurations of which they are part. People are increasingly aware of the difference lighting can make to the way a space works.

It should be clear from all this why architectural semiotics does not content itself with looking at buildings simply as physical objects or merely at the material dimensions of constructed spaces ('plastic expression').[1] It has also to take into account what we have called the 'biomatic semiotics', as well as the other semiotics listed above. But how are they

1. On semiotics as a discipline of plastic expressions, see A. Renier, in Greimas/Courtés 1986: s.v. Architecturale (sémiotique-). Architectural semiotics differs from that of other plastic expressions such as painting and sculpture, according to Renier, in that architecture (as a discipline, not as a product) has to organize space by means of mediating representations and not directly. So, whereas painting and sculpture, by large and large, work directly on a surface, architecture, like music, needs a 'score' from which to work.

all related? Renier, in his reflections on biomatic semiotics and the rest, sees them all as integral parts of a semiotics of architecture (Renier, in Greimas/Courtés 1986: s.v. Biomatique (sémiotique-) and Renier 1982: 13-14). On the other hand, he also suggests that they might be considered as autonomous disciplines related to architecture (Renier, *ibidem*). There is obviously a fair amount of interrelation and even overlap involved here, and I would propose coordinating them as follows. Taking them in sequence, from the more inclusive to the more particular, we could rank them thus:

1. biomatic semiotics
2. semiotics of spatial decoration, including lay-out, wall-coverings, paintings, etc.
3. semiotics of furnishings and appliances in the space
4. proxemics
5. semiotics of dress worn by those occupying the space, or by those passing through
6. semiotics of gesture.

Whether one sees all these different semiotics as autonomous or views them as components of a semiotics of architecture, it seems to me important to recognize that one is dealing with a syncretic (multidimensional) object. At the same time, it is important to distinguish the different dimensions and not confuse them with each other.

Thus the semiotics of architecture turns out to be a good deal more comprehensive than might at first glance have appeared. Moreover, it holds out the prospect of being able to contribute to clarifying the task and even the process of architectural design (Renier 1987: 157-174). The construction of a building, for example, clearly involves narrative programming. In fact, given the number of subcontracts and instructions, a building is the result of a multiplicity of operations, which can be regarded as so many narrative programs. These narrative programs involve numerous senders and subjects of the performance: clients, architects, contractors, designers and manufacturers of the building materials, financial institutions, and perhaps also people like politicians and government officials, architectural critics, and organs of public opinion, etc.[2] The final building is the result of many programs and anti- programs, each with their phases of manipulation, competence, realization and sanction, and each with semantic values invested in the narrative pro-

2. The complexity of the relationships obtaining between these various parties may be such as to necessitate legal action, for which rules will have to be laid down (van den Berg 1990). Here, too, semiotics could clarify what is going on.

gram. The various narrative programs can each be analyzed and their relationship to each other determined; and this could be done not only *a posteriori*, but ahead of time, to clarify relationships and responsibilities. Such an analysis would shed light on the whole planning and construction process. Once the building is completed, it may well be subjected to semiotic analysis itself, both in its syntactic and its semantic dimensions.

As an example, one could cite the *Stopera* (civic center) in Amsterdam (van Rooy and Roodnat 1986), which only finally came into being after a number of (narrative) programs and anti-programs. A national architectural competition for a new city hall was first held as long ago as 1936 and resulted in 225 entries. Two winning designs were chosen and the architects concerned were then asked to draw up more detailed plans. Those submitted by the partners Berghoef and Vegter were finally selected for the building, but the outbreak of World War II led to construction being put on hold. When they were taken up again after the War, it was decided that traffic patterns would necessitate a change of site, so Berghoef and Vegter submitted new plans. These in turn aroused so much criticism that, in 1964, the architects and the city parted ways. In 1967 a new, this time international, competition was announced, which drew 804 entries from 57 countries. A jury selected a number of finalists who were invited to submit more detailed plans, and in 1968 the Viennese architect Wilhelm Holzbauer was declared the winner. But then the Dutch government threw a spanner in the works by declaring that it would not contribute to the high costs of such an enterprise until the city could present a balanced budget. At the same time, plans for a new opera house were deadlocked. It was Holzbauer himself who first suggested combining the city hall (*stadhuis*) with the opera house; hence the term *Stopera*. So Holzbauer joined forces with the architects who had already been working for years on a new opera house, and together they came up with a new plan. In the meantime, resistance was growing to the proposed location of this new building on the Waterlooplein, which was famous for its open-air market and where many buildings would have to be torn down. Activists occupied the square and defended it strenuously, which led to several riots. The plan for the renovation of the space was bitterly contested, with the city council as one collective actor standing over against the other collective actor, the various protest groups which had emerged from the city's population. It was a clash of programs and anti-programs and their respective semantic values, as these related to the issue of how to utilize the center of a major city. Moreover, the programs relating to the designing and construction of the building itself were already fairly well advanced. Naturally, alongside the political, social and economic factors that came into play, functional and aesthetic considerations were also important, both as they came to bear on the building itself and as they related to the artistic performances to be housed there. The final phase came with the completion of the building, its outfitting and, at last, its being handed over to the occupants. This was in 1986, whereupon the sanction phase of the whole process was entered into as questions were raised about the huge cost overruns incurred by the project. This sanctioning necessitated a review of the whole building program and its countless subprograms with their respective actors, and constituted at the same time a manipulation phase in which various senders made proposals, on political grounds, for possible courses of action.

Another example might be the French supermarket that was designed to take into account the findings of a semiotic research project (Floch 1987). Local people were interviewed and it became apparent that the new supermarket was arousing two quite different sets of expectations: some thought it would be a place where shoppers could get in and out quickly, while others thought of it more as a place where people could meet. Careful semiotic analysis made it possible to design the store in such a way that both sets of expectations could be met.

It can be a valuable service to lay out the various narrative programs that a building will need to serve, as well as the relations that are to obtain between the main actants, to guide the design, construction and equipping of the building in question. Sorting out the various narrative programs and their semantic values ahead of time is most important, as well as being clear about their relationship to one another. This is equally true when a building is being treated as an *oeuvre incessante*, i.e. subject to being redefined by renovation or alteration. Especially in the case of historic buildings, it can happen that different narrative programs can get in each other's way. For example, in the case of an old house, there can be a clash between aesthetic and functional programs, where the desire for authentic restoration may well clash with the need to adapt the building to the comfort needs of modern occupants. In general, then, we can say that semiotics is in a position to contribute to improving the whole program or process of architectural planning and construction.

The semiotic approach to architectural process as it has just been outlined also offers new insight into the issue of how works of architecture can be considered works of art (Renier 1987: 157-174). Works of architecture cannot be considered the achievement of the architect – or architectural partnership – alone. Rather they are productions in which a number of participants have a hand, and the architect is simply one party with a particular role to play. Moreover, it is a fact of life in modern building that many artificial as well as natural materials are used for construction. Renier argues (Renier, in Greimas/Courtés 1986: s.v. Artificiel (sémiotique de l'–)) that artificial materials are the result of combining natural with synthetic products, these synthetic products being themselves the result of innumerable transformations. Consequently, architectural supplies are artificial products, comparable to technological products in any other field. What this means is that the artistic productions of architecture are no longer the exclusive work of architects alone. The various products of technology and engineering underline the fact that those who make them (designers, engineers, etc.) have themselves to be artists when it comes to matters of size, form, and colour. Thus the sharp division between art and science is blurred, and architecture has to enter into partnership with technology for the sake of the promise it offers in the area of artificial and synthetic materials.

This chapter has attempted to offer a general overview of the semiotics of architecture and of some of the issues that surface in it. From this it should be apparent that semiotics is uniquely placed to clarify how signification comes about in architecture. It will be the task of the next chapter to spell this out in more detail.

CHAPTER 2
Architecture and the Semiotics of
the Paris School

If one searches through the literature of the Paris School looking for definitions or explanations of the terminology as it relates to spatial semiotics in general or to architectural semiotics in particular, one will quickly find that such material of this sort as is provided is fragmentary, uneven and scattered. It seems helpful, then, to begin by pulling these materials together and to put them in order, developing the concepts where needs be and demonstrating their applicability. The goal of the exercise is to develop a methodology for analysing how architectonic objects signify. To this end, I will begin each section of this chapter by sketching the broad outlines of a semiotics of space and then move to concentrate more specifically on the semiotics of architecture. In each case, we shall follow the different components and levels of the generative trajectory and show how they pertain to a semiotics of space and to architectural semiotics.

As we start, we are immediately confronted by the fact that in space and in architecture, the generative trajectory unfolds on two distinct levels: that of the form of the expression and that of the form of the content (Hammad, in Greimas/Courtés 1986: s.v. Espace (sémiotique de l'-)). Thus it is essential to begin by exploring the difference between form of expression and form of content.

1. THE FORM OF THE EXPRESSION AND THE FORM OF THE CONTENT

Ever since the time of Ferdinand de Saussure, it has been customary to distinguish two dimensions involved in a sign: the signifier or expression and the signified or content. Louis Hjemslev refined this distinction by introducing a further distinction on each level between form and substance, yielding the following figure (see figure 1).

- The form of the expression has to do with the actual structures of the signifier. In speech, this means phonology; in architecture it means the patterned ways in which the architectural substance is constructed and recognized.

- The substance of the expression refers to the very materiality of

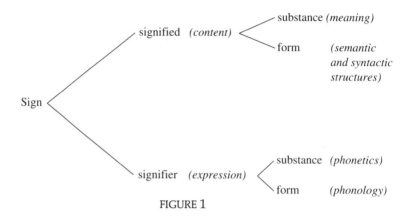

FIGURE 1

the sign. Again, in language this is a matter of phonetics, whereas in architecture we are referring to the architectural substance of the signifier in the strict physical sense. By analogy with phonetics, Levy has coined the term 'techtonics' to refer to this (Levy 1979, 1983).

- The form of the content refers to the semantic and syntactic structures that shape the sign-object.

- The substance of the content refers to the meaning communicated by the sign.

The substance of the expression can only be identified through the form of the expression; similarly, the substance of the content is only identifiable by means of the form of the content, as we shall see.

Looking at 'sign' in terms of these two dimensions raises in turn the question of how the two dimensions are related one to the other. The Paris School always sees this relationship as a relationship between the *form* of the expression and the *form* of the content. Looked at this way, three possibilities arise:

1. In what are called 'symbolic systems' the two levels are linked by forms (of expression and content) that completely match each other, so that each element of the form of the expression has a corresponding element in the form of the content. Examples can be found in formal sign-systems such as algebraic symbols, or street signs with their flashing lights, traffic signals, and pedestrian crossings. In such instances the degree of conformity between content-level and expression-level is so complete that it is hardly worthwhile or even possible to differentiate them.

2.   A second possible arrangement is represented by semiotic systems in the strict sense, such as languages. In a language there is little or no connection between the two dimensions of sound and meaning and consequently it is essential to study each dimension quite separately. This is certainly the case where 'natural languages' (as opposed to artificial languages) are concerned, for phonology (form of the expression) itself offers little or no clue to meaning (form of the content). The relationship between them is said to be arbitrary.

3.   Semi-symbolic systems – such as gesture, dress, ritual, painting and architecture – represent a third possibility. What these systems have in common is that in all of them there is some correspondence between the form of the expression and the form of the content, but it is not a correspondence between individual elements of the one and individual elements of the other, but between categories. In other words, there is a correspondence between, on the one hand, the way certain elements in the signifying form are related and, on the other, patterns of elements in the form of the content. So, for example, in the language of gesture, there is a conventional opposition between verticality and horizontality on the level of the expression which corresponds to an opposition between affirmation and negation on the level of the content. Even in language, a semi-symbolic system can sometimes be in operation, namely in poetry.

There is a tendency, in doing spatial and architectural semiotics, to concentrate too much on the plane of the expression to the neglect of the plane of content. But is it not possible that it is the plane of content that is actually more interesting and more important? Yvan Darrault, indeed, suggests that an analysis beginning with an analysis of the expression will more often than not go awry, because one is quickly overwhelmed with the enormous wealth and diversity of detail in the signifier. The goal is to link the signifier (expression) to the signified (content), but one never knows ahead of time what is important and what is not. For this reason, Darrault prefers to take the signified, the form of the content, as his point of departure, and only afterwards to examine the correlation between the two planes of expression and content (Darrault 1984: 134). Manar Hammad suggests something of the same when he talks, in reference to space and architecture, of the "heuristic priority of the content" (Hammad 1985). Without turning this into a law of the Medes and Persians, we can nonetheless agree that it is often easier, when doing architectural analysis, to begin with the form of the content. It hardly needs to be said, of course, that, just as with texts, the form of the content is not attainable except by way of the form of the expression. In this case, the form of the expression serves simply as a pointer to the content. One also needs to account for the semiosis, or process of signification, which results from the conjunction of signifier and signified, by examining carefully how the form of the expression and the form of the content are related, but this is a task best left until the end. In actual fact, semiotic analysis is usually conducted by means of a back and forth between the two planes, rather than by giving one priority over the other. The point being made here is simply that analysing the plane of the expression alone is not likely to take one very far.

Consequently, the fact that this presentation of the methodology begins with the plane of the expression is not intended to imply that the form of the expression is more important than the form of the content. On the contrary, it is only by looking back and forth between both planes that one can see which elements of the expression are actually relevant to its signifying function in virtue of being really related to the form of the content. I begin the methodological presentation with the form of the expression merely for the sake of comprehensiveness. If one were to follow this same sequence in practice, there is the danger, as Darrault and Hammad have pointed out, of doing too much. Yet the decision to proceed in this way can be justified on grounds of wishing to ensure that nothing is overlooked. In the process of developing a reliable methodology, as we are attempting to do in this book, this latter way of proceeding may also be the surer way of proceeding.

In any case, what is important to realize is that, when one is trying to analyse the signification (signifying function) of a particular, concrete object, what one is trying to do is to grasp the specific relationships that exist in this object between the form of the expression and the form of the content. For this, a merely mechanical application of methodological 'rules' will not suffice. There is no simple 'grid' that can be applied to an object that will immediately reveal the structures of its signification. Semiotic analysis is and always will be a painstaking, concrete, and yet creative process of trying to identify how a specific object (a text, a building, a rite) signifies what it signifies. In the case of spatial semiotics and the semiotics of architecture, we are dealing with an *oeuvre de significa-tion* that is the product of a manifold enunciator, or multiple enunciators. The more our analytical hypothesis (the hunch, subject to ongoing correction and modification, that governs our analysis) does justice to this *oeuvre de signification*, the closer one will come to the 'original' meaning of the work (Panier 1990: 199-220, with regard to written texts).

2. THE FORM OF THE EXPRESSION

Whenever the term 'form' is used in the literature in reference to architecture, it is invariably the outward shape of the building to which reference is being made. It is extremely important to be aware of the fact that, in semiotic parlance, the 'form of the expression' refers to something quite different. The 'form of the expression' denotes, as we have already seen, the pattern or structure by which the architectural substance is recognized and utilized. In other words, 'form' is being used here in an abstract sense to refer to networks of relationships between visual and other facets of the building, and not just to the shapes that meet the eye. 'Form', then, is not to be confused with the level of manifestation (or appearance) of a building, but consists rather in the smaller and more abstract units that go to create that appearance. So we shall continually have to make a sharp distinction between the manifest form of the expression (that which strikes the eye and which is usually what is referred to as architectural form) and its abstract forms which are what organize the various constituent elements of the plane of the expression into a network of relationships (Renier 1984: 17-18).

An important component of the semiotics of space and of architecture is the fact that we have to deal with a *plastic* dimension, just as we do in painting or sculpture. The plastic dimension consists of the materiality of the signifier (the equivalent of sound in language, for example), that is to say, the materiality of the form of expression which makes a space or a building a *constructed* space (Renier, in Greimas/Courtés 1986: s.v. Architecturale (sémiotique –)). Jean Marie Floch has described the plastic dimension as consisting of the visual qualities of the primary material used in the construction, qualities which have their own form and which can be realized in the interplay of lines and colours, of volumes and light (Floch, in Greimas/Courtés 1986: s.v. Plastique (sémiotique –)).

Defining space and architecture as plastic semiotics makes a great deal of difference in choosing a methodology for working on the plane of the expression. It enables us to avail ourselves of the work done by the Paris School, and especially by J.M. Floch, A.J. Greimas, and F. Thürlemann, in working out a method for the semiotic analysis of plastic objects other than architecture, particularly paintings (Floch, in Greimas/Courtés 1986: s.v. Plastique (sémiotique –) and Sémi-symbolique (système, langage, code –); Greimas 1979, 1984; Thürlemann 1982; Thürlemann, in Greimas/Courtés 1986: s.v. Chromatique (catégorie –), Constitutionnelle (catégorie –), Eidétique (catégorie –), Graduelle/graduable, Plastique (sémiotique –), Sémi-symbolique (système, langage, code –), Topologique (catégorie –)). I have applied this methodology to the analysis of a memorial card in *Semiotiek en christelijke uitingsvormen* (Lukken 1987 (a): 255-276).

In taking apart the plastic dimensions of the expression, two sets of categories are important: 1) the topological categories of position and orientation, and 2) the plastic categories of chromatism and eidetics.[3]

1) The *topological categories* refer to the arrangement of the plastic configurations in a given space, covering categories of position and categories of orientation.

  a. *Position* refers to categories such as the following:

    vertical vs horizontal
    high vs low vs beside
    above vs below vs beside
    right vs left
    central vs peripheral
    surrounding vs enclosed
    side by side vs opposite
    and so forth.

  b. *Orientation* refers to the direction in which things face or in which they run, such as:

    vertical vs horizontal
    upwards vs downwards
    forwards vs backwards
    linear vs circular
    branched =+=+=+=   vs layered ┬─┬─┬─┬
    and so forth.

2) The *plastic* categories in the strict sense cover two groups of features: the chromatic and the eidetic.

  a. *Chromatic* categories are those relating to colour and are manifest at least in different degrees or shades of light. Such differences of light and colour make it possible to identify the units that create significant differences (Lukken 1987 (a): 264-266).

---

3. In distinguishing between plastic categories on the one hand and topological categories on the other we have been following Greimas (A.J. Greimas 1984, notably part II, 'Le signifiant plastique'). In a later and indeed useful refinement, F. Thürlemann (F. Thürlemann, in A.J. Greimas – J. Courtés 1986: s.v. Plastique (catégorie -) rates the topological categories among the plastic categories as well, dividing the latter into constitutive categories (chromatic and eidetic) on the one hand and non-constitutive categories (topological) on the other.

b. *Eidetic* categories refer to the shape of the different units. Greimas wonders whether the most elementary level of architectural signification may not be constituted by the phemic opposition curved vs straight (Greimas 1976 (a): 147-151). At this same deep level, the oppositions circular line vs straight line and horizontal vs vertical lines may also be found. Building on these fundamental units, spatial figures such as the triangle, the square, and the circle may be developed. These figures can then, in turn, be put together in complex figures or configurations, such as the shape of the cross. By way of example, Greimas cites the George Barton House designed by Frank Lloyd Wright, as analysed by J.Castex and P.Pannerai (Castex/Pannerai 1972:79-84). In this manner, the expansion of eidetic forms, and their combination, serve to create the architectural discourse.

In reference to the discourse constituted by a piece of architecture, Greimas suggests two further possibilities. The first and more theoretical possibility is that architectural discourse is generated from a minimum of at least two independent elementary structures, so that there are contradictory codes involved. His second suggestion has to do with the complementarity of spatial figures, with some being composed of straight lines, others of curved lines. As an example of the latter, he cites the Pantheon in Paris (Greimas 1976 (a): 140).

Levy offers a broader range of eidetic architectural forms (Levy 1979; 1983). He suggests, for example, the phemic opposition /closed/ vs /open/, which could then develop into the figure of an open vs a closed square or circle. Another phemic opposition could be between /total/ and /partial/, which could then develop into the figure of a solid wall vs a wall with a window to name just one example. The list could surely be extended. On the other hand, it needs to be pointed out that Levy develops his methodology for architectural analysis rather differently than we do here. It is significant that neither Hammad nor Renier cite him, though Renier did write a review of his work (Renier 1979 (c)). In any case, it is not possible simply to combine Levy's approach with that of plastic semiotics, as defined here. We have chosen to pursue plastic semiotics because it has lent itself to the development of a practical methodology which can be applied to the semiotic analysis of actual buildings.

If we are to be able to get at how a given piece of architecture signifies, analysis of both the topological and plastic categories is essential. For one thing, it is analysis of position and the eidetic categories (which belong to the form of the expression) that makes it possible to get a clear handle on the polemical, contractual, and polemical-contractual configurations (which belong to the form of the content), as we shall see below in 3.2.1. Orientation and the chromatic categories may also be implicated.

In the case of the eidetic categories, we cited Greimas as suggesting that they may constitute the deepest level of signification, yet they were also said to be concrete. This peculiarity prompts us to wonder whether the expression plane may not consist of several levels, running from the more abstract to the more concrete on a generative trajectory, as is the case with the content plane. But we shall return to this question in n.4, below, where the relationship between the two planes and their respective trajectories will be discussed.

3. THE FORM OF THE CONTENT

In analysing the content form, we shall follow the sequence of the levels of the generative trajectory, examining each of their components in turn.

3.1 The Level of Discoursive Structures

3.1.1 *Discoursive Syntax*

Under the heading of 'discoursive syntax' come the issues of how the actors, times, and places mentioned in a text give form to its discourse. If space or architecture can be regarded as kinds of 'discourse'[4] can we also speak of such (built) space as an utterance constructed around the poles of actors, places, and times? It would seem that we can.

Actors
In daily speech we talk as if spaces or buildings or features of either were themselves actors: trees lend shade to cows; houses offer shelter and protection to their occupants; buildings beautify or mar their environment; fences surround the pasture; St. Peter's Square holds fifty thousand people; the radiator heats the room; the window sticks; the door bangs; the bench invites passers by to rest; the pulpit dominates the church; the passage leads to the kitchen; and so on. Such talk would seem to suggest that one can speak of actors even in architectural 'discourse', too.

---

4. 'Discourse' is the equivalent of 'text', as the product of human articulation. But whereas 'text' tends to be used in Greimassian semiotics to refer to the object (a short story, a painting, a building) as object of study, 'discourse' refers to the same entity insofar as it is the result of syntagmatic organization, as a rule-governed organization of significant elements.

In architecture and space, then, we can talk of enunciation and of the subjects of the enunciation, the enunciator and the enunciatee. The enunciator is a (hypothetical) 'I' who projects outside of itself various actors who in turn feature in the utterance as 'not-I'. Generally speaking, of course, these are various third-persons, in which case they are known technically as the *actors of the utterance*, as opposed to projections (thus, 'not-I') in the first and second person ('I' and 'you') which are known as *actors of the enunciation*.

It is a question whether first-person disengagements can occur in architectural discourse just as they do in literary discourse. In other words, are there actors of the enunciation in architecture, actors who are closer to the domain of the enunciation and who surface as 'I', 'my', 'our', etc.

We will want to make a distinction here between the 'I' of the client or patron and the 'I' of the builder or architect. It is remarkably seldom that buildings carry the signature of the builder. Painting and sculpture, like literature, is usually signed by the artist, whereas it is comparatively rare for buildings to bear a plaque naming the architect or the builder. It is much more common for the patron's name to be inscribed on the building, even quite prominently. On the façade of St. Peter's in Rome, for example, we find, in quite large letters, *PAULUS V BORGHESIUS ROMANUS PONTIFEX MAXIMUS*, followed by the date: *1612*. It was Paul V who instructed the architect Carlo Maderno to develop St. Peter's as a cruciform church with an enormous façade. Rome is full of buildings with such papal 'signatures', indicating which pope was responsible for the building or rebuilding and when. Very often there is also a bust or statue of the pope concerned, a practice that has lasted down to our own times. Now this sort of 'signature' is one way in which the building-as-utterance is referred back to the 'I' of the enunciator (a role usually filled by the client or patron who commissioned the work). In the church of SS. Peter and Paul in Tilburg, there is a rather unique trace of the enunciation. Among the memorial crosses for deceased parishioners affixed to the rear wall of the church, there is one with the inscription: *1900 – Johannes Lelieveldt – architect of this church.*[5]

Actually, one may question whether these instances just cited are really *disengagements* of the actors of the enunciation. It would probaly be more accurate to describe them as *engagements*, or instances in which the enunciator projects himself into the utterance in the third-person ('he'

5. The firm of architects was led by Johannes Lelieveldt (1900-1970). As the appendix makes clear the Church of SS. Peter and Paul was designed by Johannes' son: Herman Lelieveldt.

rather than 'I'). This would certainly be the case if John Paul II were to unveil a statue of himself bearing the inscription: *Ioannes Paulus II Pontifex Maximus hanc partem restauravit huius aedificii*. The examples given above are rather similar. They are so objectivizing that there would seem to be real grounds for speaking of them as engagements, rather than disengagements, of the subject of the enunciation.

Here we have been speaking of those who commissioned the work as being actors of the enunciation, but it would be interesting to push this question of the different actors further by looking at the different categories of people whose names are born by buildings. One thinks, for example, of the Centre Pompidou in Paris, the Rijksmuseum in Amsterdam, the Smithsonian in Washington, and so on, whose names bear witness to the people who commissioned the buildings concerned. On the other hand, it is rare, as we have already noted, for the name of the builder or architect to be written in stone; yet their name may be used in speaking about a building. So, for example, certain Gothic revival churches are referred to in England as 'Pugin churches' or in the Netherlands as *Cuyperskerken* (after P. Cuypers, 1827-1921). Chicago has its Frank Lloyd Wright buildings, while the Amsterdam Stock Exchange building (1897-1903) is better known as the *Beurs van Berlage* (P. Berlage, 1856-1934) and the Schroeder House in Utrecht is commonly referred to as the *Rietveldhuis* (G. Rietveld, 1888-1964).

There are also other ways, besides inscriptions and statuary, in which architects and especially the patrons of buildings can leave their mark. It is not at all uncommon, for example, in early Christian iconography, for the patron of a given mosaic or fresco to immortalize themselves by having their portrait incorporated into the artwork, even in such a prominent place as the apse of the church.

The modern development of sheathing buildings, especially sky-scrapers, with reflecting materials means that yet another form of disengagement has been developed. In this case it is the light of morning, afternoon, and evening, the different moods of the weather, the cycle of the seasons, adjoining buildings, trees, and passers-by – all disengage themselves upon the outside surface of the building as actors of an ongoing process of enunciation.

And it is important not to overlook the 'receiver' (*destinataire*) as subject of the enunciation. The receiver is recorded in such names as 'senior citizen's home', 'public park', 'police station', 'children's playground', and so on. The person or persons to whom a space or building is dedicated may also be seen in the role of receiver or enunciatee. Thus, streets, squares, and parks, as well as buildings, are commonly named after prominent individuals: the Kennedy expressway, the *Rembrandtplein*, Regent's Park, the church of SS. Peter and Paul. In such cases, the actors concerned may also turn up in the space in question in the form of a statue or other memorial.

Aspectualization of the actor may also occur. This involves having an observer envisage the actor's behaviour in relation to space and evaluate the quality of performance required. The actor may be able to proceed easily, for example, or may face a number of foreseeable difficulties; one actor may act in one way and another in another; and so on (Semanet 1987: 45). In spatial and architectural contexts similar aspectualization may well enter in, quite apart from human occupants. People speak, for example, of a heating system that is slow to kick in, of a pulpit that is easy to reach, of a window that screens the light, of a shelter that barely keeps out the cold. Similarly, in the reflecting glass of the sky-scraper, the seasons of the year and the times of the day may be aspectualized as clear, soft, changeable, and so on.

Times
Time is another of the poles which enter into the construction or organization of the discursive syntax. The enunciator in the 'now' of the act of enunciating projects times outside himself as the 'not-now' of the utterance. In spatial and architectural utterances, such time-projections are to be found whenever there are inscriptions giving the date or the year. Such information represents a temporal disengagement of the utterance: for example, the date inscribed over the door of a house, or on the foundation stone of a major building, or even in some countries, the practice of naming a square or street after a significant date, such as the *plein 1944* or the *rue 14 juillet*. One would have a temporal disengagement of the *enunciation* if the inscription read "Now..." or "On this day..."

A totally different form of temporal disengagement turns up, once again, in buildings that reflect their surroundings. The 'now' of the time of day or the season of the year is disengaged upon the building, which is thereby linked to time.

It seems rather problematic to look for *temporal aspectualization* in architecture, but it does occur. Temporal aspectualization is involved when an observer sees purely logical narrative functions (arriving/departing, giving/receiving, having/losing, etc.) in terms of a temporal sequence with a beginning, a middle and an end. By analogy, an observer could equally well see a long staircase or a wide expanse of open floor in terms of 'durativity' (length of time needed to negotiate the space) or a revolving door in terms of 'iterativity'. Once again, reflecting buildings offer a particular form of aspectualization as they manifest the inchoativity of morning, the durativity of daytime, and the terminativity of evening, not to mention the iterativity of people mirrored coming and going.

Places
It is only to be expected that it is the spatial dimension which attracts the most attentions in architectural 'utterances'. In such utterances, the 'I' located 'here' disengages places which represent a 'not-here'. This usually means a simple spatial disengagement of the utterance, but there are instances where a spatial disengagement of the enunciation may also come into play; if, for example, there were an inscription that read: "Here on this spot, on this the 8th day of October 1988, NN., who commissioned this building, formally opened it." In an inscription of this kind, the architectural utterance is linked to the 'here' of the enunciation. A similar sort of spatial disengagement of the enunciation can also occur with respect to the user (enunciatee), as when an inscription relates the building to the one (or those) for whose use it is built: "Hic domus dei est" or "Terribilis est locus iste."[6] There can also be enunciative disengagements of space where buildings reflect their surroundings.

The Paris School goes on to differentiate three kinds of spatial disengagement of the utterance, namely: (a) spatial localization; (b) spatial programming; and (c) spatial aspectualization. We will take each of these in turn.

(a) *Spatial Localization*
Spatial localization occurs when a 'ground-zero' is established in reference to which all other places are situated. This 'ground-zero' thus represents a point of departure and is called the 'topic space'. Surrounding areas (even if behind or in front of the 'ground-zero') are known as 'heterotopic spaces'. Thus, in the case of a spatial discourse such as a town or a building, the town or house in question is the 'topic space' and the surrounding areas of towns, villages, squares and streets, are 'heterotopic'. Within the topical space, a further distinction can be made between 'utopic' and 'paratopic' areas. The utopic space is one in which a particular performance takes place; for example, a museum when it is visited, a city square when sightseers flock to it, and a restaurant when people are dining there. The paratopic spaces are those in which competence is acquired for the performances undertaken in the main (utopic)

---

6. "This is the house of God" or "Awesome is this place."

space: for example, if the sightseers rest up awhile in a park; or the super-market where food is bought and the kitchen where it is prepared before it reaches the restaurant (Semanet 1987: 45-46).

(b) *Spatial Programming*

There is spatial programming whenever there is a syntagmatic or sequential stringing together of subspaces in view of the spatial localiza-tion of narrative programs. If we return to the examples just mentioned, the supermarket, the kitchen are paratopic in relation to the dining room, and the park where people can rest is paratopic in relation to the main program of sightseeing. Paratopic places are places where so-called 'aux-iliary' narrative programs are performed, enabling people to acquire the competence they need for the main narrative program in the utopic space (Greimas/Courtés 1979: s.v. Spatialisation and Programmation spatio-temporelle; Semanet 1987: 46).

(c) *Spatial Aspectualization*

Spatial aspectualization occurs whenever an actant-observer transforms the action of a subject-actant into a process occuring in space, such as bodily movement, exploration, surmounting of obstacles, etc. (Bastide, in Greimas/Courtés 1986: s.v. Spatialisation, par.2, and Aspectualisa-tion, par. A1 and A6). In so doing, the observer acts as an anthropo-morphic standard, lending a human scale to what unfolds in space. Thus the observer might look at the location of objects from the vantage-point (*aspect*ualization) of the physical distance to be crossed between them. Or their location could be assessed in terms of their accessibility to the different senses. If it is a matter of seeing, touching, smelling, or hearing, we can speak of the cognitive dimension of spatial aspectualization, as opposed to the pragmatic or somatic dimension. In aspectualization, therefore, an observer is always installed to offer a vantage-point from which these things are assessed and does so as representing the average person.

As far as the pragmatic dimension of spatial aspectualization is con-cerned, if two points are situated at a distance from each other, the observer will be able to register program from one to the other in terms of setting out (inchoative), progress along the way (durative) and arriving (terminative). In a journey of discovery, for example, there will undoubt-edly be emphasis on the (terminative) arrival at the desired destination, but it is also possible that the story could be told in terms of the durative character of the journey there, or even in terms of the inchoative experience of setting-out. Conversely, in the story of the exodus of the Hebrews from Egypt, the terminative is aspectualized (end of slavery), whereas in the account of their arrival in the Promised Land, it is the inchoative (new beginnings) which is accented. Similarly, in a church building, one might think of a procession as inchoative (entry procession into the church), as terminative (the recessional out of the church), or as durative (a procession round the church). On the other hand, a dancing pilgrimage such as that at Echternach might be characterized more by its iterative aspect, as the same steps are repeated over and over again. Aspectualization is also involved when we look at a building's entrances (inchoativity) and exits (terminativity), or when a building is only partly finished, as is the case with the cathedral of Beauvais (incompleteness). A typical example of the latter is, of course, the Jewish synagogue which is usually left partly unfinished to symbolize our incompleteness as creatures over against the perfection that belongs to Yahweh our creator.

The distance between two points can also be expressed figuratively by means of a wall or other obstacle dividing the separate areas. The wall that used to separate East from West Berlin would be one example; the labyrinth that the hero had to negotiate to reach his goal in ancient tales would be another; the roodscreen or iconostasis marking off the area reserved for the clergy from the rest of the church would be yet another.[7] One might also think of the various kinds of spaces that often have to be traversed by a visitor to gain access to some inner sanctum, as in the palace at Versailles, where one can only reach the most important rooms after walking a considerable distance.

It is also frequently the case that spatial aspectualization has less to do with actual physical or pragmatic movement than with access from one point to another by means of the other senses: sight, smell, hearing, or touch. The actant-observer will note that, confronted by a solid wall, a subject of the performance cannot see the place that is his eventual destination or experiences it as inaccessible. Thus, in terms of spatial aspectualization, one can distinguish, for example, between a solid wall and a trelliswork. Both represent pragmatic inaccessibility, but a solid wall also rules out any glimpse of what lies beyond it, whereas a trellis sets up a certain tension between cognitive accessibility (where the eye can go) and pragmatic inaccessibility (where the body cannot go). Spatial aspectualization also permits us to make distinctions between subjects (or objects) which are immediately touchable (inchoative), those which are out of reach (terminative) and those which can be held and touched over a period of time (durativity). Similary with hearing: sounds from the next

---

7. The roodscreen is a carved screen, surmounted by a large crucifix, placed across the entrance to the choir or chancel in medieval Western churches. The iconostasis is an even more solid screen, covered with icons, which performs the same service of separating the clergy from the laity in Byzantine churches.

room may be immediately audible (inchoative), or totally inaudible (terminative) or continually audible (durative). Likewise with odours and the sense of smell.

Françoise Bastide remarks that in differentiating between places in terms of the total sensorium (sight, touch, sound, smell) the visual is usually dominant. In other words, spatial differentiation is invariably figurativized by the presence or absence of an obstacle to seeing such as a horizon or a wall (Bastide, in Greimas/Courtés 1986: s.v. Spatialisation, par.A3). In this way, opposition is created between what is 'inside' and what is 'outside', an opposition which entails a further opposition between subjects and objects that are present or absent. Here we see emerging already on the discoursive level the syntactic component of the surface or semio-narrative level; for the presence or absence of a subject and object in a given room (discoursive level) can be homologated with the relations of conjunction and disjunction between subject and object at the surface level. Conjunction is then figurativized as the simultaneous presence of a given subject and a given object in a given space, while disjunction appears as the simultaneous presence of a given subject and a given object in different spaces. So spatial aspectualization serves to qualify the manner of their conjunction or disjunction. An object can be very close to a subject, within a hand's reach; or it can be further away, fully perceptible, but not attainable without the subject's moving. Relationships of conjunction and disjunction can also be aspectualized on the discoursive level in other ways. For example, tensitivity can by figurativized by a face peering through a window: the transparency of the window allows the subject to be visually conjoined to the value-object located outside, but the glass of the window at the same time represents an obstacle to complete pragmatic conjunction or to conjunction by means of touch.

The predominance of the visual over the other senses in spatial aspectualization may well be a cultural phenomenon. Such, at least, is the opinion of Christian Metz, who argues that in our Western tradition vision takes priority in any ranking of perception, followed by the auditory and the tactile, with taste and smell coming in last (de Kuyper 1986: 122). It is striking that the Greimas/Courtés dictionary has no entries for aspectualization by taste or smell.

Important developments and perhaps corrections in relation to aspectualization and the senses are to be found in Greimas' later work *De l'imperfection*, where he speaks of visuality as the most superficial of all the senses. Taste and smell, he argues, create a more intense level of conjunction between subject and object. And he points out the importance of the sense of smell for communication with the holy – 'the odour of sanctity' – as well as for contact with the devil, whose presence is traditionally signalled by sulphurous fumes (Greimas 1987: 71-78).

Enunciation
The term 'enunciation' has come up a number of times already, and it seems appropriate to examine the concept a little more deeply.

The term itself is borrowed from linguistics. In the works of Greimas it is used in two related ways (Greimas/Courtés 1979: 125-126; Lukken 1989 (c); Metz 1988: 54 ff.; Panier 1991; Simons 1988: 89 ff.). On the one hand, enunciation is used narratively, in which case it refers to a performance. In such a performance, the virtual semio-narrative structures, which constitute a subject's semiotic competence, are actualized on the basis of the deep level in the direction of discourse, the generated product. So conceived, enunciation is both a production and a transition from a virtual to a realized instance. On the other hand, 'enunciation' is also used by Greimas to refer to the *mise-en-discours*, or turning into discourse effected by the instance of the enunciation. This instance of the enunciation is the partnership of enunciator and enunciatee which is logically presupposed by the existence of any utterance. It is particularly this latter understanding of enunciation that has previously surfaced in our discussion of actors, times and places as enunciative disengagements.

It is important not to confuse this usage of 'enunciation' as effecting a *mise-en-discours* with the pragmatic understanding of the terms as referring to the act of speaking where *empirical* subjects engage in intersubjective interaction. As used in semiotics, the enunciator and enunciatee are merely *logical* (and not empirical) subjects, who exist merely as presuppositions of any utterance. They are only recoverable by means of such traces of the enunciation as may be left in the discourse. Enunciator and enunciatee are therefore strictly abstract structural instances which are not to be confused in any way with the empirical sender (author) or receiver (reader). Unfortunately, it is all to easy to conceive of enunciator and enunciatee as some kind of persons. As Metz warns, the very terms 'enunciator' and 'enunciatee' tend to acquire anthropomorphic connotations just in virtue of their suffixes. This is unfortunate, for it makes it difficult to separate the term enunciation from a linguistic context. All too easily, enuciator and enunciatee are enfleshed as an 'I' and a 'thou' located at a particular place and time. So, even though these subjects are not empirical, it is hard not to imagine them as such. Nonetheless, it might be possible to break away from this imaginary speech situation if the enunciator is thought of as the 'seed' or 'source' of the enunciation, and the enunciatee as its enunciative 'goal' or 'target', its enunciative purpose or orientation. When enunciator and enunciatee are understood in these terms, it is easier to see how they can also be used of non-linguistic texts, such as space and architecture.

Perhaps this account of the concept of enunciation can help clarify some of what has been said above. For one thing, it will not be surprising that those for whom the building is designed and constructed can also be seen as embodying the role of subject of the enunciation. Just as the enunciator is not to be identified with the author of a text, so neither is the enunciator to be identified with the architect of a building. After all, the 'clients' can also be part of the domain of the enunciation if the latter is seen as a *mise en espace* or a *mise en architecture*, the act of uttering an idea in space or in architecture. But, if that is so, then the question may be raised whether or not the issue of enunciation was not approached too linguistically in what was said above. For, in fact, in the case of architecture the domain of the enunciation can also consist of physical things, not just people: the tools and techniques used, building codes, and so forth. A building will often show signs of being made of prefabricated components which presuppose, in turn, a certain embodiment of the domain of the enunciation. There may be a bricklayer's handprint, or a characteristic style to the way the stones are cut; or stamps or marks impressed in brick which are signs of a particular manufacturing process or of the fashion of a particular time period; there may be so many technical traces of the building process itself, or of economies made at the time. We can therefor ask what the source of the architecture might be. But we can also ask what traces are left by the enunciatee. The role of enunciatee is played in a certain sense by anyone who looks at the building or uses it, but it is also represented by the express destination or purpose of the building: it is a 'public building' or 'a church', or a building for 'outsiders' rather than 'insiders', or whatever. Generally speaking, the enunciatee (or purpose) of a bungalow will be substantially different from that of a church building. In the latter case, the intent will be to gather a whole congregation under one roof, whereas a bungalow will be designed to ensure an optimal level of privacy for one family.

3.1.2 Discoursive Semantics

In discoursive semantics, a very important distinction is drawn between figurativization and thematization. Figurativization is connected to the figurative function of an utterance, that is to say, to the fact that an utterance points to the extralinguistic world of experience. Figurativization has to do with the organization (or form) of the content of the utterance insofar as this organization or form relates to our world. Thematization is quite different. It is also part of the form or organization of the content, but in terms of the intentionality or angle of approach which the utterance adopts towards the world of which it speaks. Now we need to take figurativization and thematization in turn and see how they work out in relationship to architecture.

Buildings and other constructed spaces are dressed out in a whole host of elements which point to the world we already know. So it is, for example, that we are able to recognize a constructed landscape as either a park or a garden. Various parts of a town can be identified as a square, a parking lot, a harbour, and so on. We can 'recognize' the materials and characteristic shapes of buildings. So spatial utterances are organized and structured in a particular way precisely in view of their reflecting the world we know; and it is our knowledge of these forms – or discursive memory – which enables us to identify the figurative organization of an actual building or other spatial object in concreto. Taking architecture specifically, the important question to ask is whether any architectonic micro-narratives (configuration) are evoked by the architectonic utterance (building) in question and, if so, how they are uniquely reproduced in this utterance as a figurative trajectory.

So, for example, the architectural utterance may call to mind such configurations as those of a palace, a castle, a church, a factory, or a domestic residence, for example. And the trajectory can be much more detailed if, to take the residence as an example, it gets down to such paradigmatic distinctions as between bungalow, cottage, multi-storied house, apartment, and so on. Similarly, architectural micro-narratives are possible in the interior of a house with its different rooms: separate living rooms or 'open plan' interiors, however the various spaces are differentiated; but also bedrooms, hallways, passageways (straight or labyrinthine), access from inside to outside, different rooms linked to each other by connecting doorways, and so on. And on top of all this there is the matter of style, such as romanesque towers, gothic arches, or baroque façade.

A specific and particularly intense kind of figurativization is what is known technically as iconization. This is when the figures of the utterance are so developed that they come to resemble the realities to which they refer and create a strongly representational image. In linguistic discourse, this occurs by means of concrete references to places (toponymy), persons (anthroponomy), and times (chrononymy). In architectural utterances, the same 'reality-effect' can be created in different ways, all forms of inconization. For example, a church can be designed in the form of a tent, or the nave can be made to look like a town square. But iconization is also at work when buildings are designed to look like other buildings. Clear examples of this latter phenomenon are to be found in the church of St.Peter at Oudenbosch (Netherlands) or the much disputed basilica of Our Lady of Peace at Yamassoukro (Ivory Coast), both of which are reproductions (the first small-scale, the latter large-scale) of St. Peter's basilica in Rome. A milder form of iconization occurs when churches are built in the so-called 'neo-' styles: neo-gothic, neo-romanesque, neo-classical.

In trying to identify a text's figurative trajectory (and its thematic trajectory, for that matter), it has usually been found useful to put several heads together. In group work, the different insights and suggestions offered represent so many hypotheses concerning possible figurative trajectories in the discourse. The same is true for identifying the figurative trajectories (and the thematic trajectories, of which more later) in an architectural utterance. Here it is often helpful, also, to consult whatever documentation there may be concerning the building, such as architects' briefs or reviews, which may suggest hypotheses which can then be tested against the building itself.

Thematization
Thematization has to do with the answer to the question: in virtue of what thematic value or values do these figures have their place in this discourse? From what particular angle does this discourse view the world of experience as this is reflected in its figures? What, in other words, are the thematic trajectories?

Similar sorts of questions can be posed with regard to actual architectural utterances. For example, a courtyard: does it thematize privacy, inaccessibility, and hiddenness versus openness to the public, accessibility, and visibility? And a drawing room in a private house might thematize 'Sunday use' versus 'everyday use', or 'for visitors' rather than 'for family'.

The search for figurative and thematic trajectories in a building is complex. It is not enough merely to take into account the spatial arrangements alone. Figurative and thematic trajectories can also be determined, for example, by the way people act to occupy the space (proxemics), or by the way light, sound, smells, or decor are distributed. Space, after all, is a syncretic object. The moment all the light in a room, or in part of a room, is concentrated on one person, this person becomes the center of the room, even if, in geometric terms, he or she is off to one side. The same would be true if that person's voice were more easily heard than others', whether because of the building's acoustics or because of a sound system. Written signs on a building may also contribute to its syncretism. So a bar or restaurant might proclaim itself as "Albert's Corner", thereby suggesting that the place is invested with certain thematic role (cosiness, informality). Or a house might bear the name "River View". Whether or not the buildings concerned live up to their billings and fulfil these thematic roles depends in large part on the architectural form of the expression, and it is to be expected that, when analyzing space as a syncretic object, one will sometimes come across thematic trajectories that conflict with one another. It is important to be alert for such complexities. On the other hand, it is also important to differentiate the manifestation languages very carefully, so that the consequent analysis can be as exact as possible. For now, however, it will suffice to emphasize the fact that in doing a semiotics of space we are dealing with a syncretic object. For the sake of clarity in the analysis itself, it is usually best to begin by focussing on the space itself, including the way the light falls and the play of colours (the visual elements of the space), and the objects that are placed in that space. With regard to the objects themselves, it is best at first merely to note their location and general design, but not, at first at least, to get involved in an analysis of the objects themselves. In any case, given the present state of development of this method, it is necessary to accept some limits to what is attempted.

In analyzing space, there is a second problem that arises: is a building or space to be analyzed in terms of the use for which it was designed (and which the space itself might be said, therefore, to intend) or in terms of the use to which it is actually put? In the latter case, it is less a matter of an occasional departure from the original purpose, but more of adapting to an established pattern of altered use. Such adapted use may depart significantly from the usage which the space itself proposes, in which case there is an actual signification quite different from the signification originally intended. As we have already remarked, such new usage often prompts a renovation or reconstruction of the space in question. In short, it may be necessary to differentiate as many as three situations: that of the original building, that of the adapted building, and that of the renovated or reconstructed building.

Figurative and Thematic Isotopies
Just as it is possible, in analyzing literary discourse, to comb through the various figurative and thematic trajectories looking for the dominant connecting threads, so too with buildings. What is at stake here is the figurative and thematic isotopies respectively of the architectural utterance.

3.2 The Surface Level

The surface level, despite its name, is a level that is more abstract than that of the discoursive structures and lies, as it were, even deeper below the level of the discourse's manifestation. And just as, at the discoursive level, a distinction is made between discoursive syntax and discoursive semantics, so too the surface level has both a syntactic and a semantic component.

Claude Zilberberg has pointed out that it is difficult to think of the narrative surface level, with its relationships of conjunction and disjunction, other than in spatial terms. Similarly, the deep structures themselves are difficult to imagine except in a spatial schematization displaying both the fundamental semantic and the transformations (operations) which constitute the basic syntax (Zilberberg, in Greimas/Courtés 1986: s.v. Spatialisation, par.B). But since these structures do not in fact occupy space, and since the opposition space/non-space (like time/non-time) makes little sense, he proposes instead the opposition figurative space vs figural space. This opposition is to be understood structurally, i.e. with figural space being a constant and figurative space being a variable.

What Zilberberg's observations undoubtedly show is that neither the surface level nor the deep level can be thought of except in quasi-spatial categories. Thus the conceptual framework for both these levels has to be both temporal and spatial.

The relevance of this approach for our more specific enterprise in spatial semiotics is that it indicates at how fundamental a level spatial categories are operative: even when thinking in highly abstract terms, spatiality still plays an important role. Nevertheless, Zilberberg's insights are not particularly relevant to our purpose, since it contributes nothing to a semiotics of space as such.

3.2.1 *The Syntactic Component*

As Françoise Bastide points out, a distinction can be made between subjects and objects that are present in a space and those that are absent (Bastide, in Greimas/Courtés 1986: s.v. Spatialisation, par.A3). With this distinction, we arrive at the syntactic component of the surface level, since the presence or absence of subjects and objects in a given space indicates relationships of conjunction and disjunction obtaining between these subjects and objects. Conjunction means the simultaneous presence of subject and object in the same place; disjunction indicates the simultaneous presence of subject and object in different places.

The surface level in relation to space and especially to buildings, has been further explored by Manar Hammad (Hammad 1979 (a) and (b), 1983, 1984, 1985, 1987, 1989; also in Greimas/Courtés 1986: s.v. Espace (sémiotique de l'-)). Those responsible for constructing a building equip that building, in part at least, with syntactic roles. The division of space in terms of roles creates what is known technically as the 'topos'. These 'topoi', equipped with syntactic roles, are thereby enabled to participate in the various narrative programs like any other actants: they can play the actantial roles of sender, receiver, subject of the performance, subject of state, modal object, value object, and observer. We can therefore speak of the immanent organization of the space, in virtue of which the space itself is a means of communication and brings about signification, independently of the actors that enter that space (Hammad 1989: 1). So, for example, segments of the space can habitually exercise the role of **sender**. This role is delegated to these topoi by the (collective) sender of the space. For example, a town architect or an office of urban planning, in cooperation with the town council, will already have determined which topoi will exercise a manipulative role in the town and will let them exercise that role in accordance with whatever conditions were decided. In actual fact, our whole environment is full of such senders: innumerable signs along the roads and in the towns, traffic signals, barricades, traffic islands, pedestrian crossings, speed checks, neon advertizing, billboards, escalators, and so on. The roads themselves are senders, as are bicycle paths, sidewalks, squares and parks, all of which govern the ordering of space and thus determine our socio-cultural relationships. Similarly, within a building there are any number of senders: the front door, the hallway, the hatstand, the garage, the living rooms. On a recent visit to the theater in Tilburg, I was struck by the way the red carpet and the broad staircase and even the design of the ceiling, manipulated visitors to move slowly in a certain direction, beyond the cloakrooms and on towards the main auditorium.

All the topoi such as those we have named have been delegated as senders to manipulate the **receivers**. These receivers may include other topoi. For example, a wooded section of a park could be considered a topos in which, in the fall, the birch trees manipulate the production of fly agarics (poisonous mushrooms) while other kinds of trees manipulate a topos of edible mushrooms. In similar fashion, the roundabout is a topos manipulating the roads around it; a main street manipulates the side streets; and so on. And, of course, delegated senders can manipulate human actants as well: the open gateway to a park communicates to receivers a 'being-able-to-enter', a 'knowing-how-to-enter' and a 'being-allowed-to-enter'; the barrier at the frontier or on the toll-road permits the driver to pass, but only on certain conditions; a bench in a shady spot in the park plays the actantial role of sender in relation to a virtual narrative program in which a receiver might be prevailed upon to sit down and relax.

Topoi can also serve as delegated **subject of the performance**. In an industrialized environment such as ours, the topos of the central heating system is a delegated subject of the performance of conjoining all the different rooms (**subjects of state**) with the value of warmth, via the topoi of the radiators. The same can be said of the working of automatic pilots. computers, and robots. And the different topoi where the processes are monitored may be credited with the actantial role of **observer**.

Hammad points particularly to the fact that topoi can play the actantial role of **modal object**. This occurs whenever there are specific modal values or competencies associated with a place. So a certain hierarchy or configuration of adjoining topoi can be associated with a corresponding range of competencies attributed to the actants who occupy those different places. The respective topoi manipulate those conjoined with them by equipping them with certain performative modalities: of having-to, being-able-to, wanting-to or knowing-how-to-do. On a soccer pitch, for example, there are at least two topoi: the pitch itself and the stands. Each topos has its own very different competencies: the pitch gives the competence to play soccer, the stands give the competence to watch the game. Between these two topoi, there is a topos for the trainers and substitutes, and there is even a special topos reserved for photographers. Another example would be the arrangement of the topoi of teacher and students in a classroom: the topos of the podium and the topos of the blackboard, and the seats or benches for the students. This arrangement indicates the manipulative role of the two topoi with regard to the receivers who conjoin themselves with these topoi as with modal objects which are mutually related. Conjunction with the respective topoi determines the modal competencies of having-to, wanting-to, being-able-to, and knowing-how-to-teach (the topos of the teacher) and having-to, wanting-to, being-able-to, and knowing-how-to-learn (the topos of the students). Moreover, in a school building such modal relations are strongly regulated by the overall lay-out of the various topoi: the principal's office, the staff room, the student areas. It is important to note, though, that in all these cases, the modal values are not attributable to a single topos as such, but that we are dealing rather with a double arrangement or configuration: a topical arrangement and a modalizing arrangement. The topical arrangement properly belongs to the form of the expression, whereas the modalizing arrangement belongs to the content form. In short, we are dealing with a semi-symbolic system.

As delegated senders, the topoi not only regulate modal relationships between human actors themselves, but also the modal relationships between human actors and their environment. In this way, the topoi can be so arranged (topic configuration) as to control the modal relationships of human actors to such things as light, air, heat, the street, the city, the landscape. It may be that light, air, heat, the street, the city, the landscape are unable to connect with the enclosed space in which the human actor is found. Thus the topoi control the modal relationship between what is 'inside' and what is 'outside'.

Entering into the topoi and assuming the modal values associated with them always implies a fifth modality, namely, the shared acceptance of such conventional communication. In other words, there is an implied fiduciary contract concerning the mutual relationship of the competencies in question. But the actual and presumed competencies associated with the topoi rest upon social convention and/or regulations, whether these are made explicit or remain merely understood. So, for example, the competence which is associated with a given place can be derived from one person's repeated occupation of that space: over and over again, students in seminars tend to sit in the same place until the point is reached that they expect that place to be saved for them. In a family, members usually occupy the same seats from one meal to the next, so that the father's place or the mother's place comes to be associated, by dint of repeated occupation, with the competence of a certain right. Hammad cites the example of a table in a dining hall at which, during a convention, the leaders of the convention are accustomed to sit together. It quickly becomes a "table de pouvoir" and it would be found very disturbing if, without warning, other people started sitting there (Hammad 1984 and 1989: 31ff.). Thereafter there is an implicit rule that 'this is now the custom'. Here the sender is social life with all its pertinent conventions. In virtue of such social convention, repetition of patterns of behaviour give rise to a certain 'have-to-do' which constitutes an actual contract. A *de facto* right is established, as opposed to the *de jure* right deriving from the rule that whoever is the first to be conjoined to a table or chair has a right to that place: the right of the first claimant. In both instances we are dealing with implicit contracts, as a result of which, in a situation where conflict arises (the son sits in his father's chair), one right has to yield to the other, or at least negotiation has to take place (Hammad 1989: 31-32). If, as a consequence, the son regularly begins to sit in his father's place, a new right arises *de facto*; which suggests, in turn, that the foundational contract is only maintained if it is periodically renewed in practice.

Competencies are differentiated from one another by a **boundary**. Such a boundary may be simply imaginary, as in the example just given of someone having their own chair or their own place at table. Similar imaginary boundaries may also occur in topoi that have to do with 'public' and 'private' space. For example, if one person comes visually too close to another, the bounds of privacy are overstepped. Such overstepping of bounds is only tolerable if there is a previous agreement as to the intimacy of the relationship (Hammad 1989: 75). For similar reasons people can begin to feel uncomfortable if they are crowded together in a public space, as sometimes happens in modern churches when the seats are locked into each other. Another example is when people enter a fitting room in a clothing store to try on clothes, only to find it equipped with a television camera to prevent theft. And when a group of people stand around in a circle in the foyer of a theater during the intermission, they thereby create a private topos, in contrast to the public space all around them. It would be considered an invasion of people's privacy if someone were to break into the circle, or wander nonchalantly through the middle of it. In this latter case, the wall of backs is what constitutes the imaginary boundary between public and private space (Hammad 1989: 36). It can only be broached if certain conditions are fulfilled, namely if the newcomer is part of the circle of friends or acquaintances.

But the boundary between topoi can also take any number of physical forms. Through this range of options, architecture is able to give expression to the conditions attached to boundary-crossing (Hammad 1989: 35). The frontier between countries can be marked by boundary markers and barriers, but it could also take the form of a Berlin wall. There is quite a difference between a high, solid wall, a fence, and a wall built of glass partitions. Each of these govern the different modalities in different ways. In discussing spatial aspectualization we have already made a distinction between spatial aspectualization in the pragmatic or somatic dimension and aspectualization of the cognitive dimension. It is important to come back to the subject here in connection with the modal object. A solid wall controls modal relationships both in the cognitive and in the pragmatic dimensions: what lies beyond the wall is physically and cognitively inaccessible, at least to those standing on this side of the wall. This could be the expression of a modal relationship in relation to a given area which for one actant is accessible and for another actant inaccessible. At play here is the modal relationship of not-being-able and not-having-to. The modal relationship will be different, however, if it is a matter of a fence with railings, or of a partition with peep-holes. In this case, there is still physical inaccessiblity, but the other side is no longer visually inaccessible. In light of this, it is very understandable that foreigners who are used to having their houses screened off with walls are taken aback to be able to look so easily into so many Dutch homes from the street, especially when it is dark out. A very particular kind of boundary, comparable to that of the barrier, is the door, which is in some sense part of the wall. According to Hammad, walls serve to dissuade those approaching a building from entering it, requiring them to look for a door or gate through which it is possible to undertake the crossing of the boundary (Hammad 1979 (a): 25-27; 1987: 6; 1989: 40). The condition for being allowed to and being able to enter the house through the door or gate without further ado may be that one is the owner or leaser of the house. So the door represents a boundary between what is one's private domain (permanently in the case of the owner, temporarily in the case of the lessee) and the public domain. The door is thus a divider between two spaces, in each of which different competencies and different semantic values prevail: the space outside the house is associated with the semantic value 'public', the inside with the value 'private'. A guest will be invited into the house by the owner: that is to say, the owner of the house lends the guest the competence to enter. But even once the guest is inside the house, there remain differentiations between the different rooms of the house. Perhaps the guest will only be let into the hallway; or maybe the host will invite the guest into the living room, or even show him over the whole house. This implies that even within the house there are various kinds of boundaries, pointing to a hierarchy of competencies and to the even more private character of certain rooms within the home. Only when a person has the free run of the whole house is he really 'at home'. The narrative program of the burglar, illegally going from room to room, is clearly a total invasion of privacy. Very often, then, the boundaries are tightened after a burglary. The potential burglar is manipulated by an alarm system, or breaking in is made more difficult by the addition of extra locks and other security devices (Lukken 1989 (b): 28-29).

There are also many different ways in which architecture can set boundaries for non-human actors in the environment (Hammad 1989: 41-42). A breeze, for example, can be let in or kept out of a house depending on whether the windows are opened or closed. A closed window will admit light to a room while excluding fresh air, insects, and odours. A wire gauze can let in fresh air but not insects. In this respect, the Pantheon in Rome is very interesting. Because the keystone, as it were, is missing from the apex of the dome, all sorts of combinations of sunlight and air quality are possible inside the building. Thus, it is possible to envisage all sorts of selective boundaries that can be erected to exclude or admit various natural actors.

The boundaries set around a given topos can either be permanent or temporary. In some instances, permanent or long-lasting conjunction with the topos may well be excluded, while temporary conjunction is permitted (Hammad 1989: 73 ff.). For example, someone might well conjoin himself or herself with the front door (public topos) of a private house, in order to ring the doorbell, or to check out the name plate, but is not allowed to stand there for a long time. The kind of topos that is a front door is a public area, but only for a limited period of time. It serves as a kind of transition area between public and private realms. The same might be said of the 'regular' seats in a dining hall or lecture room. They have the character of a private topos, but only for the duration of the meal or the lecture, and revert to public status as soon as the session is over. Similarly, it is perfectly in order for an outsider to sit in the seats of the Members of Parliament, or on the front bench, or even in the Speaker's chair, as long as Parliament is not in session. This goes to show that space is not an entirely timeless matter: time is tied up with it, as are actors. So space, time, and actors need to be seen as three closely related elements. They are, as Hammad points out (Hammad 1989: 74), the three components of discoursivity.

Boundaries can thus serve as **senders** with regard to various different **competencies**. In working on the semiotic analysis of a building, it is very important to be on the look-out for boundaries that can only be crossed conditionally, and to identify the conditions for crossing them. Boundaries are always an indication that the spaces they differentiate are associated with different competencies. So relational roles, with their reciprocal competencies, are invariably marked off topographically. In this way, the same spaces may have a double role as sender: insofar as they are differentiated from each other, each topos is sender of the corresponding topos; but each space also plays the role of sender to those who are conjoined with it as with a modal object. This shows just how close the link is between space and social life, so that one could say that spatiality, or architecture, is the spatial expression of social life (Hammad 1989: 72). So space is much more than just circumstantial, more than just a necessary backdrop to the realization of actions. Rather, it is a particular and special dimension in which social relationships develop and come to full realization (Hammad 1989: 77).

There is a further remark to be made concerning the role of space as sender. We have already spoken of architecture as an *oeuvre incessante*, as never finished, always in process. Because of this, it is always possible that those actually using a building may override, negate, or alter the original, 'in-built' sender, so that it now functions differently. A hat-stand, for example, may no longer be used, but be preserved instead as an historical relic, a monument, or a piece of ornamentation. If such an object still has a sender role at all, it may well be no more than that of sender of a program of remembering the past, or of aesthetic appreciation.

Finally, topoi can also function as **object of value**. A subject of a performance might envisage a conjunction or disjunction with regard to a particular topos: to enter a park, to travel to a city, to leave a building/In such cases, these places function in the role of object of value. In this respect it has to be noticed that topoi may also assume the actantial role of spatial object of value by means of the modal values conjoined to them. Then they are objects of value which carry with them various modal values. In other words, competence can be looked at as an object of value, with which the subject of the performance conjoins itself as a subject of state. So, for example, the teacher's podium carries the modal value of being-able-to-teach: only someone who is authorized to teach can stand at this podium. But the podium is also a value-object, to which the teacher repeatedly returns in order to teach. As such, it implies such value-objects as the qualification to teaching, the office of teacher, and so on. This is even more the case in those instances where the first conjunction with a topos is deemed to require an installation or enthronement, as is the case with the enthronization of the king on the throne or of the bishop on the cathedra. It is through the first (solemn) conjunction with such spatial objects, that the actor concerned actually assumes the office of king, bishop, or whatever. After this performance the throne and the cathedra act as objects of value with reference to kingship and episcopacy.

Hammad offers a brilliant analysis of how, even in the context of friendship, there is often a symbolic exchange of each other's topoi (Hammad 1989: 51 ff.). The host welcomes his friend and offers him his own particular chair (topos) to sit in as a place of honor, while he himself sits in some other place. And when the visit is returned, the ritual is repeated, meaning that there is a mutual exchange of topoi as value-objects, implying mutual investment of the modal value of being-able-to-use the space (known in the vernacular as 'making oneself at home').

In considering the roles of topoi as senders, objects of value, and modal objects, **three topical configurations** are particularly significant: the polemical, the contractual, and the polemical-contractual or contractual-polemical (Hammad 1984, 1987, 1989; Lukken 1989). In each case, it is a matter of a semi-symbolic match between the form of the expression and the form of the content: the relations existing between the topoi on the level of the expression form correspond to the relations between the topoi at the level of the content form.

a. *Polemical Topical Configuration*
The topical configuration or structure we call 'polemical' occurs[8] when

---

8. The terms 'polemical' and 'contractual' are purely descriptive and are not, of themselves, indicative of any positive or negative values.

each actant is located in a topos confronting the other. When this happens, the respective topoi exercise a manipulative role with regard to the actants occupying them, so that their relationship is modally asymmetrical or polemical. The result is that the respective topoi function as bearers of modal values (competencies). And as bearers of modal values they may function as objects of value too. This kind of arrangement is one that can be visualized as allowing no room for overlap between the sharply differentiated areas of topos 1 and topos 2. It can take a number of forms, as the following illustration demonstrates:

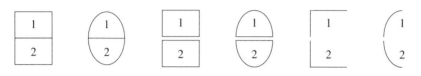

FIGURE 2

Such topical arrangement is seen most clearly in time of war between two nations. Under such circumstances, the one topos is most emphatically forbidden territory for those who belong to the other topos. Frontiers are carefully guarded and anyone crossing from one topos to the other will automatically be regarded as carrying out a hostile anti-program. Another example would be the strict compartmentalization of social life in the context of a class-ridden society, where the workers' residences are topologically set apart from the mansions of the factory owners. In this instance, topology itself would assume a polemical character, perhaps with the railroad tracks as boundary.

There is also a polemical arrangement when wild animals are locked up in cages. Only the animal tamer can overcome the polemical character of this arrangement, as when he goes into the lion's cage and works to establish a relationship with the beast. But there are other, less dramatic instances of polemical configurations, for instance where there is simply a program and an anti-program which find spatial expression, as in the goals at opposite ends of a football field. And finally there are polemical arrangements that are even less confrontational, where competencies are simply complementary and, in that sense, mutually exclusive. An example would be that of the teacher in front of the class, or the lecturer before an audience, or the monarch presiding at the opening of Parliament. Very often, spatial configurations in a building merely reflect such differences of competence and serve in that sense to determine social relations. For this reason, it would be wrong to understand the term 'polemical' as necessarily implying any kind of hostility, but rather as indicating 'over against' each other and reciprocally excluding one another.

b. *Contractual Topical Configuration*
A topical configuration or structure is contractual when there is a ring or square with an empty space at the center. Such a configuration brings those who join themselves to it into a contractual modal relationship with each other; so the ring or square can also function as a value-object invested with contractual modal competence. This sort of topical configuration is repeatedly found in all cultures and can take any of the following forms:

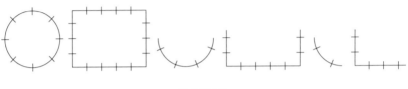

FIGURE 3

c. *Polemical-contractual or Contractual-polemical Topical Configuration*
A polemical-contractual or contractual-polemical configuration is one in which two different topoi, each with its own pole or point of orientation, are juxtaposed, but with an empty space in the middle. A classic example of this arrangement is the space prepared for the Japanese tea ceremony, in which the guests' topos (T1) has its own pole consisting of a piece of calligraphy or a flower (P1), while the host's topos (T2) has the fire as its pole (P2) (Hammad 1987: 29-31). This arrangement can be diagrammed as follows:

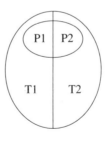

FIGURE 4

The polemical-contractual type of configuration is also realized in the case of a circle with a pole functioning as its center. One might think of a circle with a person or object standing in the middle, as when a crowd gathers around to hear a speaker or to watch some work or other in progress. A variation on this configuration is found when, in a square or a ring, an explicit topos is left for another pole; for example, when a seminar meets, but a place is reserved for the professor to sit at (Hammad *et al.* 1979: 49-50). Such configurations manipulate the actors to modal relationships of a polemical-contractual kind, and can also function in the actantial role of value-object, to which subjects conjoin themselves with a view to assuming the appropriate modal relationships. A range of topical configurations falling under this category are represented in figure 5.

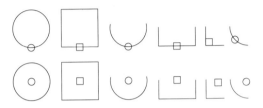

FIGURE 5

It should be apparent from the diagrams presented above that, in polemical-contractual configurations the emphasis can be put either on the contractual or on the polemical: hence it will be seen as either contractual-polemical or as polemical-contractual.

It should be clear from what we have said how very important built space can be in facilitating human communications. Connected with this is the fact that relationships between people – as well as between people and things – are governed not merely by what people say, but by what they do and the place in which they do it (Hammad 1987: 6). The built space makes a fundamental contribution to the way people define themselves in relation to each other and helps shape those relationships as contractual, polemical, polemical-contractual or contractual-polemical. From a semiotic perspective, then, architecture has the ability to manipulate and control interpersonal relations. It plays the role of a delegated subject and, as such, it is taken up and integrated into the interaction between two actants. These actants can be collective, as in the domestic residences of the near and far East, or as in public buildings in general. The topical configurations determined by the architecture introduce the actants who occupy the space to stable modal relationships and the alteration of such patterns of relationship is not at all easy. Often enough, it only happens at the expense of conventional behaviour, if not of good manners or even ethics. If, for example, an ordinary citizen were to manage to seat himself on the queen's throne at the opening of Parliament, this would be regarded as an outrageous breach of modal relations. A comparable incident did occur at our university (the Catholic University of Brabant) back in the sixties, when a number of students disrupted the opening of the academic year by wearing handkerchiefs in lieu of academic bands and sitting between the rector magnificus and the emeritus professors, facing the assembly, and trying to initiate informal conversations during the proceedings. In the home, a comparable act might be sitting in father's chair, a clear breach of modal rules. Similarly, bedrooms in a house are not interchangeable, and the parents' room in particular will usually have its own modal rules. The very fact that one can speak of a parental bedroom is often determined by the architect who provides just one room with the means to be locked from inside.

Hammad remarks on the strange fact that there is only a small number of topical configurations and corresponding modal relations even across as wide a spectrum of cultural styles as Japanese, Syrian and European architecture. And that is not all, for the same topical configurations function in the same way in locations that, on the face of it, seem entirely different: the private residence, the university, the theatre, the stock-exchange, and the church.

Finally, actantial roles can be defined in terms of programs that are themselves hierarchically organized. The order of senders and subjects established by delegation can be studied as sequences of manipulation: a) the primary or original sender of the building is the architect, the client, and so on; b) the topical configuration of the building itself, as fixed by the original sender, becomes a first delegated sender; c) more specific indications in the topical configuration, introduced by the people actually using the building, represent a second-level delegated sender. As for relations with the elements, a similar sequence of delegations can be established. For example, a) the client, architect, builders, etc., are the original senders; b) the way the building configures its light (by means of windows, etc.) constitutes a first delegated sender; c) a shade or blind introduced by the occupant is a second delegated sender; d) additional lighting, designed to illuminate dark corners and to add to the light coming from outside, would be a third delegated sender.

3.2.2. The Semantic Component

We saw above that topoi can function as objects of value when the subject of the performance enters into a relationship of disjunction or conjunction with such a topos. As we turn now to the semantic dimension of the surface level, the question arises of identifying the semantic values (the smallest identifiable signifying units, or classemes) which are invested in the spatial value object. Here a number of possibilities arise.

Someone might go to town, for example, in order to take a walk, or to do some sightseeing, or to go shopping. One could buy a house simply as a place to live or one could buy it in order to have somewhere to entertain. Moreover, in our discussion of the syntactic dimension, it was pointed out that modal values, too, can be associated with topoi. Putting all this together, it is apparent that conjunction with a topos as value object may be for the purposes of acquiring the modal semantic values associated with it. In other words, it may well be the modal competence associated with a topos that constitutes the semantic investment of the object of value. So, for example, a king might take his place upon his throne simply to lay claim to his authority as leader. The same could be said of a bishop taking his place upon his cathedra.

There is yet a third possiblity, namely, that in the conjunction of a subject and a topos the spatial dimension of the topos itself could serve to bring additional semantic investment to the topos as value-object. One can illustrate the point by recognizing that not all thrones are of equal value. A throne could be designed as lofty and remote from the common people or, conversely, it could be made deliberately simple and accessible. The same could be true of the lecturer's podium: it could take the form of a high, elaborate tribune or be nothing more than a table where the students can crowd around. These examples underline the fact that very many different kinds of spatial discourse are possible and that spatial value-objects expressing the same modal competence are capable of being invested with a range of different semantic values depending on how they are presented spatially. In the case of the throne or podium, the higher versions might well be bearing values such as /closed/, /high/, /exclusive/, and /single/ while lower versions might be associated with the values of /open/, /low/, /inclusive/, and /joint/. These values would then be filled on more concretely by the figures and themes of the discoursive level, for it is on the discoursive level that such abstract oppositions as /open/ vs /closed/, /high/ vs /low/, /exclusive/ vs /inclusive/, /single/ vs /joint/ are fleshed out in specific designs. A bishop's cathedra, for example, might take the form of a chair fitting into the figurative trajectory of 'household furniture' and into the thematic trajectory of 'closeness' and 'simplicity'; quite different from the sort of cathedra which belongs to the figurative trajectory of 'king of the castle' and might thematize 'feudalism'.

Finally, a fourth possiblity arises in the context of the polemical, contractual, and polemical-contractual or contractual-polemical configurations. The very indicators that suggest which kind of configuration is realized in any given instance already point to the direction in which the semantic investment is tilted: polemical, contractual, polemical-contractual or contractual-polemical. Nevertheless it is very important to try to determine as precisely as possible from the concrete discourse what those semantic values are. In the case of the polemical configuration, for example, oppositions such as /equality/ vs /inequality/, /friendship/ vs /hostility/, or /togetherness/ vs /isolation/ may be operative.

Pertinent semantic values, then, are invested in the topoi. As such, it is a matter of actualized values. On the other hand, when the values in question are not merely associated with the value-object but are in fact conjoined with or disjoined from a subject, then we are talking of realized values. And finally, when the values are considered in detachment both from the subject who may acquire them and from the value-object in which they might be invested, we have to speak of them as merely virtual. But, in that case, we are already at the deep level of the generative trajectory, and it is to that that we must turn next.

3.3 The Deep Level

At the deep level, we deal with the question of what the final elementary structure governing the signification of a particular discourse might be. This elementary structure of the signifying process can be laid out on the so-called 'semiotic square'. Just as on the other levels of the generative trajectory, so here, too, there are both semantic and syntactic components. To the semantic component belong the virtual values mentioned above. These are the smallest identifiable units of signification (the classemes), and they can be set out on the four corners of the semiotic square. However, the square does not merely lay out to view the reciprocally related classemes: it also identifies the operations that transform them. In this way, the semiotic square is able to indicate how, in a particular discourse, the transition from one value to another takes place. As far as the relations are concerned, the semiotic square is static, but when it indicates the operations, it is as it were set in motion. The relations are what constitute the elementary semantics of the discourse, the operations its elementary syntax. The spelling out what it means to use the semiotic square in reference to architecture will be left to section 4, following.

4. RELATIONSHIP BETWEEN THE FORM OF THE EXPRESSION
   AND THE FORM OF THE CONTENT

As we have already noted, space and architecture are semi-symbolic systems in that the relationship is always between patterns of relationship on the expression level and patterns of relationship on the content level.

The question now is whether it is possible to operationalize the relationship between expression form and content form in any greater detail. Manar Hamad has written, "Il y a plus: le fait que le plan du contenu s'analyse en différents niveaux (profondeur, surface, manifestation) induit une analyse du plan d'expression en différents niveaux d'abstraction" (Hammad 1983: 29). Elsewhere he has also remarked, "Enfin, l'analyse de l'expression spatiale se fait a différents niveaux d'abstraction, montrant qu'il y a lieu de considérer un parcours génératif également sur le plan de l'expression. La mise en relation des parcours des deux plans permettrait peut-être de caractériser ces sémiotiques d'une façon formelle, amenant ainsi à en modifier la dénomination" (Hammad, in Greimas/Courtés 1986: s.v. Espace (sémiotique de l'-)).

As we saw earlier, Greimas – in the context of a discussion of the architectural expression – speaks of the phemic categories of curved vs straight as the most elementary level of architectural signification, out of which the figures and configurations are developed on a more concrete level (see above, p.27).

The literature, therefore, seems to indicate that that there are several levels on the plane of the expression, too, and that it should be possible to bring the generative trajectory of the expression plane into correlation with that of the plane of the content, as in figure 6.

Expression	*Content*
Deep level	Deep level
Surface level	Surface level
Discoursive level	Discoursive level

FIGURE 6

However, the literature of the Paris School offers no examples of such homologation in reference to architecture, nor any further indications on how it might be done. The only person to have made any sort of attempt in this direction is A. Levy (Levy 1979, 1983), but his approach is rather complicated and somewhat artificial. The approach we offer here, on the other hand, seems more easily integrated into Greimassian semiotics.

Greimas himself actually offers a more detailed way of proceeding, at least with regard to a linguistic expression form and a linguistic content form, in his work on poetic discourse (Greimas 1972: 14). In the case of poetry, Greimas argues, there is a certain isomorphism between the form of the expression and the form of the content. He presents this isomorphism in the following chart:

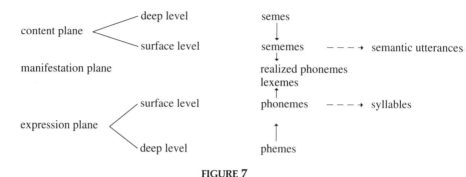

FIGURE 7

Note that this isomorphism is not a term-to-term homologization whereby a phonomatic unit on one plane would correspond to a semantic unit on the content plane of a poetic piece. If that were the case, we would be dealing with a symbolic system, in which each element of the expression plane has its corresponding element on the content plane. Here, in contrast, we are dealing with the kind of correlation that can best be expressed as syllable 1 : syllable 2 :: semantic utterance 1 : semantic utterance 2 (which is a semi-symbolic relation). This is on the surface level, of course. The analogous correlation at the deep level would be pheme 1 : pheme 2 :: seme 1 : seme 2 (Greimas 1972: 14-15).

In this article, Greimas has not yet come to make the distinction between the discursive level and the surface level. If we take that distinction into account, we end up with the diagram on the next page (figure 8).

On the deep level, it is a matter of semes and phemes, which are virtual classemes and virtual contextual phemes which play out against the unvarying background of the virtual nuclear semes and virtual nuclear phemes. On the surface level, the nuclear semes and classemes, the nuclear phemes and contextual phemes undergo actualization and become sememes and phonemes. On the discursive level, these sememes and phonemes are realized and take on the guise of the figures of the content and the figures of the expression.

Though it is developed to account for the isomorphism of linguistic forms of expression and content, this model can well serve for use in reference to architecture. But it does raise the question of whether the terms 'pheme' and 'phoneme' are appropriately maintained in architectural analysis. Greimas himself has admitted that the use of the terms 'pheme' and 'phoneme' can only be confusing when used outside a linguistic context (Greimas/Courtés 1979: s.v. Figure), for they are, of course, borrowed from linguistics. The concept of the phoneme, particularly, was

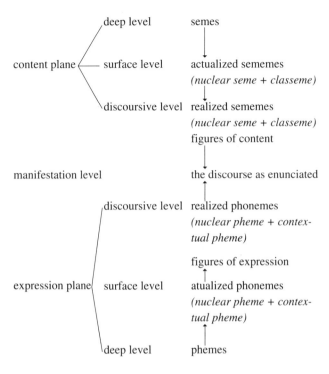

FIGURE 8

developed to denominate the *sound*-signifier found in natural languages (Greimas/Courtés 1979: s.v. Figure and Phonème, par.1). This prompts Levy to plead for the use of alternative terminology and, by analogy with phonology, phonetics (see Figure 1) and phonemes, he proposes 'tectonology', 'tectonics', and tectonemes (Levy 1979: 8, 89 ff; 1983: 1-2). However, Greimas himself speaks of 'phemes' even in discussing architecture, as we saw. He also makes the point that the procedures that lead to the elaboration of the phoneme "have a general value and can, if needs be, be applied to other types of signifiers (graphic, for example) and to other semiotic systems" (Greimas/Courtés 1979: s.v. Phonème, par.1). For this reason, I am inclined to hold on to the terms 'pheme' and 'phoneme' even in analyzing architecture. It is true that the terms have their origin in linguistics, but they are nonetheless of broader applicability. And such extensions are commonplace in the Paris School: one has only to think of 'enunciation', 'enunciator', 'enunciatee', and 'utterance'. These and similar concepts have become accepted and it seems better to adhere to one and the same metalanguage across the various semiotics.

Having said all that, it is important to return to the diagram given in Figure 8 and re-work it more specifically for architecture.

On the deep level of the form of the expression we encounter contextual and nuclear phemes. Greimas suggests that the most elementary phemes are 'circular' or 'curved'/'straight' and 'horizontal'/'vertical' (see above p.27). He seems to depart from one of the plastic categories in particular: the eidetic expression forms. I have already shown that the topological categories of location and orientation and the plastic category of chromatics are also important in the context of the form of architectural expression. Both on the deep level and on the surface level, we find such phemes as high/low/sideways, above/below/beside, right/left, central/peripheral, embedding/embedded, side-by-side/opposite, upwards/downwards, forwards/backwards, linear/circular, branched/layered, light/dark, black/white. To this list, Levy suggests, we ought also to add such phemes as open/closed and whole/partial (Levy 1979, 1983).

On the surface level, the phemes are actualized as phonemes by being conjoined with actants such as object of value, subject of performance, and so on. Here one can think of such nuclear semes as the square, the triangle, and the circle and of the contextual oppositions which play against the 'background' of these nuclear semes.

On the discoursive level, realized phonemes are concretized in such figures of the expression as 'house', 'upstairs' and 'downstairs', 'annex', 'main room', 'siderooms', 'bedrooms', 'living room', and so on.

To substantiate the theory, we can take a classic example of the polemical topical configuration. In the Netherlands, at the opening of parliament, it is customary for the queen to give an address before a joint session of both chambers. To do so, the queen and her consort take their seats on a dais which is higher than the floor of the chamber where the members of parliament are seated.

If we begin with the form of the expression, we can see that on the discoursive level the dais and the chamber constitute figures of the expression. They represent two square areas, one larger, one smaller, confronting each other, with the smaller square (the dais where the queen and her consort sit) raised higher than the larger one assigned to the parliamentarians. Here we have what we might call a realized phoneme: a small but higher square versus a larger but lower square, with which the queen (and her consort) and the members respectively are conjoined. In other words, there are both nuclear phemes (square shapes) in different sizes and also contextual phemes such as high vs low or opposed vs juxtaposed. On the surface level, the same nuclear phemes and contextual phemes recur, but now as actualized. Finally, on the deep level, the contextual phemes low vs high and juxtaposed vs opposed play against the 'background' of the nuclear phemes straight (rectangular) and quantitative. This can be displayed on the semiotic square:[9]

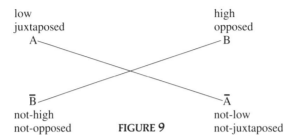

FIGURE 9

Turning to the form of the content, there appears to be a figurative isotopy of proxemic relationships, on the discoursive level, and a thematic isotopy of polemic relationships. On the surface level, we can identify nuclear semes such as spatiality, relation, and relationship, together with the contextual semes or classemes /inclusive/ vs /exclusive/ and /equal/ vs /hierarchical/. If all this is then taken to the deep level and laid out on the semiotic square, we get the following diagram of the form of the content:

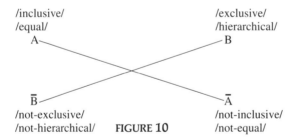

FIGURE 10

The form of the expression and that of the content are so matched at each level that the relations identified on the plane of the expression can be homologized with those identified on the plane of the content. For example, the two semiotic squares can be laid one over the other so that the phemes high vs low and juxtaposed vs opposed are isomorphic with the classemes /inclusive/ vs /exclusive/ and /equal/ vs /hierarchical/. If it should ever happen that the queen would first seat herself on the front bench and then move from there to the throne, we would have an

9. The dash over the letter A expresses negation, so non-A. Similarly, the dash over the letter B forms the standard notation of non-B.

instance of the operation from A through Ā to B. And if an additional space were provided beside the throne for the ladies-in-waiting, a space somewhat lower than the queen yet higher than the members of parliament, such a place could be located on the semiotic square – both from the point of view of the form of the expression and from that of the form of the content – in position Ā.

This serves to show once again that the plane of the expression and the plane of the content can only be related semi-symbolically. It is a matter of analogous patterns of relations found on each of the two planes, not of direct relationship between specific elements of one plane and corresponding elements of the other. Perhaps one last example can serve to make the point more clearly. 'Maranatha' is the chapel for students in Tilburg. The interior is so arranged that the faithful sit higher than the ministers, as if in an amphitheatre. In this instance, the relations high vs low on the plane of the expression contribute to the signification in a way which is the inverse of the last example, for they correspond to the opposition /inclusive/ vs /exclusive/ on the plane of the content.

A complete isomorphism between the content and expression planes in linguistic texts only occurs, according to Greimas, in the most perfect poem, a poem that would be a poet's *cri du coeur* (Greimas 1972: 23). Such an ideal seems unattainable, and the same is probably true for a building. The closest one would come to it would be one in which there was a high degree of isomorphism between the two planes: the building as successful poem. But, in architecture as in poetry, the perfect match of expression and content remains an ideal after which to strive, though it never be fully realized.

CHAPTER 3
The Semiotics of Church Architecture

Anyone wondering about the state of the question in liturgical studies regarding liturgy and space would be well advised to turn to recent manuals as a starting point (Lukken 1989 (b)). The Italian manual *Anamnesis* (Marsili *et al.* 1974) nowhere mentions the relationship of space to ritual: it simply omits any treatment of the church building or its furnishings. Moreover, the section on "liturgical hermeneutics" deals exclusively with principles for interpreting liturgical texts (Augé/Civil, in Marsili 1974: 159-207), thereby overlooking all the non-verbal dimensions of the liturgy. The French publication, *L'église en prière*, has a section entitled "Principes de la liturgie", in which there is a chapter on signs, among which the church building, the altar, the baptistry and the churchyard are all covered in an isolated way in a scant ten pages (Martimort 1983, I: 210-220). Otherwise, the matter of the liturgical space is barely mentioned in passing (Martimort 1983-1984). On the other hand, a number of new insights with relation to the non-verbal elements of the liturgy are offered in the German *Handbuch der Liturgiewissenschaft* and especially in the volume on the *Gestalt des Gottesdienstes* (Sequeira 1987 (a): 7-39). Here Ronnie Sequeira expands upon the themes of liturgy as "menschliche Ausdruckshandlung" and notes that, hitherto, the study of liturgy has been almost entirely confined to the study of its words and music, with practically no attention paid to the kinesthetic dimension of human expressivity (Sequeira 1987 (a): 24-26; 1987(b): 7-39). Sequeira sketches in broad outline the research undertaken in this area and shows that, even since Vatican II, few works have appeared "die sich um eine übergreifende systematische Darstellung der Bewegungsdimension und um entsprechende begriffliche Klärungen bemühen" (1987(a): 25). He goes on to propose a system and a technical vocabulary for the study of movement but, as he does so, it becomes apparent that one fundamental dimension of liturgical performance – its spatiality – is once more to be left aside. Furthermore, he proposes to treat the dimension of liturgical space (together with iconography, liturgical vessels and liturgical vesture) quite separately from the verbal, musical, and kinesthetic dimensions of the rite. He writes: "Da der liturgische Raum eigens behandelt wird (s.u. 6 und Teil 8, 534 B: Kirchweihe), können wir uns hier mit einigen Hinweisen begnügen. Der liturgische Ausdruck sowohl der Heiligung des Menschen als auch der Gottesverehrung entfaltet sich notwendigerweise im Raum. Die räumlichen Bedingungen sind daher eine *wesentliche sekundäre* Ausdrucksdimension, insofern sie dem *primären* Ausdruck in Wort-, Klang-, und Handlungssymbole *ermöglichen und mitprägen...* Was soeben vom Raum gesagt wurde, gillt – mutatis mutandis – auch von all jenen Dingen, welche wie jener das räumliche *Umfeld* der liturgischen Feier *mit*bestimmen..." (Sequeira 1987(a): 19-20, emphasis added). One may conclude that, while Sequeira recognizes the importance of the language of space he undervalues it as a secondary dimension of the rite in comparison with other basic forms and fails to include it in his "übergreifende systematische Darstellung". Sible de Blaauw is right in remarking that systematic studies integrating architecture and Christian liturgy are few and far between (de Blaauw 1991: 1).

In his attempt to systematize the dimension of movement in liturgy, Sequeira touches briefly on semiotics. He writes: "Man muss allerdings darauf hinweisen, dass auch die Semiotik bisher selten auf andere als sprachliche Ausdrucksformen einging und ihre Methoden nur aufsatzweise für die Untersuchung non-verbaler Ausdrucksformen in Ansprach genommen sind" (Sequeira 1987(a): 26). Insofar as this judgement purports to be a verdict on semiotics in general, it is simply wrong: contemporary semiotics is certainly not confined to verbal manifestation languages, but is actively engaged in analysis of non-verbal languages. On the other hand, as a verdict on liturgical studies, it is undoubtedly correct, for such semiotic studies of liturgy as have been undertaken have tended to confine themselves largely to analysing verbal texts. It is important that liturgical studies should develop ways of analysing the semiotics of non-verbal manifestation languages, for liturgy is more than a text serving as script or scenario which is then dressed up in other languages at the time of performance. Just as in theatre studies (see, for example, Pavis 1976), so in liturgical studies the conviction is growing that the subject under investigation is a complex syncretic object in which any number of manifestation languages are interwoven with each other and contribute together to the overall signifying function of the object.

It became obvious in the previous two chapters that the semiotics of architecture plays a basic enunciative role in human communication. In inescapable ways, it governs the reciprocal relationships of human beings, as well as their relationship with the environment. In the case of liturgy, it is certainly my impression that the ritual space is even more determinative of people's relationships with each other and with the environment than is ordinarily the case. For in rituals relations are regulated by means of spatial senders in a very stable way. This would be true for all ritual; for, if it is the case that the spatial, and especially the architectural, dimension is an integrating and fundamental dimension of human communications strategies, that is even truer of the communications patterns of ritual. The space itself, as it is divided up and furnished, is a constitutive part of the narrative program of the rite. Or, to put it another way, the spatial senders influence the actors of the ritual: they determine their relative competencies and the specific semantic investments of the ritual. This makes the spatial-architectural dimension of ritual a part of the ritual that has particular importance for integrating the rite as a whole. Failure to take the spatial dimension carefully into account in analysing a rite can only result in an incomplete picture of what is going on. A crucial element has been lost. In fact, the spatial-architectural dimension is so important that this is where one should always begin in observing and analyzing a rite. Convincing proof of this claim is to be found in a few concrete analyses of ritual, particularly those done by Manar Hammad of the ritual of greeting a guest in a Japanese house, of the Japanese tea ceremony, and of the privatizing (in the semiotic sense) of space (Hammad 1979, 1987, 1989).

At this point in time we do not have any semiotic analyses that use the conceptual apparatus of the Paris School to analyse the spatial and architectural dimensions of Christian liturgy. (For an initial foray in this direction, see Lukken 1989(a)). Part II of this book will undertake such an analysis, but it seems as well to preface that undertaking by concluding Part I with some general remarks about the semiotics of church architecture.

Let us take as our point of departure the kind of church building that developed in the Catholic Church between Trent and Vatican II. Generally speaking, it was a style characterized by the way it drew a sharp dividing line between the church as such and the area surrounding it. In the ecclesiastical architecture of this period, to enter the church is to cross a rather clearly defined threshold. It is true, of course, that the doors constitute an invitation to enter, but they are cautious in doing so, for only very rarely are they wide open and beckoning. Often, to reach the nave, the visitor will have to pass through one or more transitional spaces. At either side of the entrance, holy water stoups manipulate the visitor to perform a rite of purification: crossing oneself with holy water. The interior of the building is conceived in opposition to the space outside the church, for the purification rite, which is a condition of entry, bespeaks a transition from the profane to the sacred. Once inside, the interior seems subject to similar topological differentiation (Lukken 1990). There is a nave which is clearly separated from the sanctuary by a visible barrier. Interestingly, the separation of the two areas is pragmatic, but not cognitive, for the church offers a vista stretching all the way to the far wall of the apse. The division is somatic. First of all, there is a communion rail which either runs unbroken across the width of the sanctuary or else has a gap in the middle closed by a gate. Second, the boundary between nave and sanctuary is marked by the fact that the sanctuary is elevated above the level of the floor of the nave. Within the sanctuary, the centremost and highest point is the altar. The boundary between nave and sanctuary can only be surmounted in virtue of ordination: only consecrated persons may penetrate into the sanctuary. Thus the arrangement of the interior space of the post-Tridentine church manipulates the actors and determines their respective competencies in the rituals celebrated there. The clergy have the competence of being-able-to-act inside the sanctuary, whereas the laity have no competence to cross the boundaries that define the nave as their area. Actions that are specifically sacred all transpire within the sanctuary and the laity can never become subjects of the performance in that space. Thus, the church building which is marked as sacred over against the profane space that surrounds it, is itself divided into a less sacred, or sacred-profane, area (the nave) and an exclusively sacred area (the sanctuary).[10] The faithful usually approach the sanctuary for holy communion. The communion rail is so designed that it keeps the laity on the outside of the sacred space and manipulates them to kneel down. On the other hand, the priest at the distribution of communion operates from the other side of the rail – the sacred side – and does so standing. With the competencies thus divided, the performance of the distribution of communion unfolds, with the priest as subject of performance, the laity as subject of state, and the eucharist as object of value. So the communion rail operates as a sender, clearly determining the respective roles of the actors at this high point in the Mass.

The rubric in the marriage rite of the 1614 *Rituale Romanum* is also of interest here.[11] According to the directions given by the rubric, the couple to be married are to take up their place "in aliquanta ab altari distantia seu ante presbyterium" ("at a distance from the altar, or in front of the sanctuary"). In other words, from the vantage point of the altar, they are to keep their distance, while from the vantage point of the nave they are to stand at the boundary that marks the beginning of the sanctuary. This positioning corresponds precisely to the physical lay-out of the church. Like the rest of the congregation, the bridal pair stays out of the sanctuary, but it comes as close to the sanctuary as it can without actually crossing the threshold. Moreover, the area of the sacred is indicated by reference to its center point: the altar. Thus this spatial narrative program of the altar provides the basis for everything else that is to unfold in word and action. Detailed semiotic analysis of the mar-

10. Interestingly enough, a similar instance of 'more or less' also occurs in the topology of the Japanese tea ceremony. See Hammad 1987: 23-27.
11. For an analysis of this ritual, see Lukken 1987 (b).

riage rite of the 1614 *Rituale* reveals that the bridal couple do in fact act in giving their assent ("I do"), but that this performance only pertains to the juridical – one might say, the profane and exterior- dimension of the marriage rite. It is more of a preconditional program which equips the couple (competence) for the real performance which constitutes the definitive and existential core of the sacrament, namely, that of which the priest is the (delegated) subject of the performance. Standing at the edge of the sanctuary, or inside the communion rail, he carries out the main performance as an instrumental subject of the divine, saying: "I join you together in holy matrimony. In the name of the Father and of the Son and of the Holy Spirit. Amen." Bride and groom are clearly nothing more than the receivers of the sacred value-object, the Christian marriage bond, which the priest confers upon them. Thus the manifestation language of space and architecture and the manifestation language of word and action correspond very closely to one another (Lukken 1987 (b)).

There are also a number of other senders in church interiors dating from the Trent-Vatican II era which have been delegated by the builder and which shape the programming of the ritual. For instance, when the faithful enter the church, they genuflect. They are manipulated to do so by the sight of the tabernacle and the lamp burning beside it, which indicate the invisible presence of the eucharist (the hosts being enclosed within the tabernacle). Another sender is the pews, which are designed for sitting and kneeling. In addition, the liturgical ritual itself contains a number of actions which are governed by spatial senders: the priest's genuflecting before the tabernacle, kissing the altar, the movement from the Epistle side to the Gospel side of the altar, the movement to the pulpit to preach, to the sedilia for the priest or to the throne for the bishop, and so on. Conjunction with the altar, the throne, the pulpit is always an expression of modal competence, while the actual concrete form assumed by these furnishings in any given instance may well add a surcharge of such semantic values as 'exclusivity' or 'authority'. For there is an unmistakable difference between a lofty, enclosed pulpit and a simple lectern, or between a grandiose, elaborate throne and a simple chair. It should be added, of course, that time is also a factor, for the bishop's throne and the pulpit are really only 'off-limits' during the time of the service. Outside the times of services, visitors are often free to wander around, sit on the throne and mount the pulpit. And the more secularized a society is, the more this time element will play a role.

In some cases the church is divided by the presence of a roodscreen.[12] When this occurs, semiotics can offer a highly nuanced analysis of the

12. See note 7 above.

spatial program by having recourse to the concept of spatial aspectualization. A rood screen certainly represents somatic inaccessibility, but it
does not altogether bar cognitive access to what lies behind it. It thus sets
up a certain tensitivity, since the sacred actions can only be glimpsed in
the distance. Similarly with the iconostasis of the Eastern churches,
which plays a very important role in programming the Divine Liturgy.
Careful analysis would reveal all the different nuances that are possible,
given the presence of the holy doors in the icon screen, as well as the curtains that can be closed, thereby cutting off access to the eye but permitting the ear to continue to follow the action. Of similar interest, in Western churches, is the variety of ways in which the inaccessibility of the
tabernacle is expressed: locked doors, open doors but closed curtains,
curtains open, transparent tabernacles, and so forth. A very particular
kind of tensitivity is to be found in the way the host is kept behind glass
in the monstrance: the subject is visually in contact with the value-object,
while remaining physically separated from it, insofar as he or she is in a
separate space from which the object of value can be seen but not
touched. The impossibility of a genuine pragmatic conjunction by means
of the sense of touch is also found in the case of relics behind glass: the
faithful can kiss the relics and touch them, but not directly. Given all
these possibilities, it is possible to categorize them in terms of objects that
are directly accessible to touch (inchoative) or objects – such as candles or
palm fronds – that can be held for a shorter or longer time (durative), and
objects that are either untouchable or barely touchable (terminative).
Among the latter we would have to count certain consecrated vessels, the
consecrated host, and the host or relics put behind glass.

As we remarked earlier, it can happen that the actual users of a space
override some of the senders present in the space. When that happens,
the ritual is obviously no longer governed by these senders and by the
programs in which they were originally intended to function. So, for
example, it can happen that the holy water stoups at the back of the
church are ignored, or that the side altars are no longer used, or that no
one ever preaches from the big pulpit any more. When that happens, the
former senders of ritual programs become no more than monuments to
past practice. They could be retained for just that reason, as manipulating to a program of activity directed to the past, or as monuments inviting an aesthetic program. Or perhaps they are removed altogether, and
then we are confronted with the problem of the renovation of ancient
church buildings, where liturgists and art historians, each pursuing their
own programs with their own sets of values, all too easily come into conflict. A classic example of this was the renovation of the church of St. Ser-
vatius in Maastricht (Netherlands), where the ritual program several
times ran into conflict with the aesthetic and art history programs, par-

ticularly with regard to some neo-gothic paintings. From a liturgical point of view, it was thought best to remove these paintings altogether, but this only roused the ire of those who wanted to maintain as much of the neo-Gothic decor of the building as possible (Blijlevens et al. 1983). So careful planning of the different narrative programs with their different semantic investments and careful coordination of the different actants in the process is just as necessary in the case of renovation as it is in the designing and constructing of church buildings. In either case, it is certainly desirable that, in programming the process, room be left for the mediation of liturgical studies and of the Church's liturgical law.

After Vatican II, liturgical space underwent considerable alteration. The boundaries that marked off the building from surrounding space were altered, and with them their corresponding semantic values. On occasion, glass walls were even used to link the interior of the church with the outside world, while entrances were usually made more accessible. In short, the dividing line between the church and the outside world was no longer as important as it had been. Semiotically speaking, there is a considerable distance between the solid door, characteristic of old churches, which visitors had to open for themselves, and doors that either simply stand open or else open as each visitor is welcomed to the church. In each of the three instances, there is the competence to enter, but only in the last two instances is there really an explicit invitation to enter. The arrangement of the church interior has also changed since Vatican II (Lukken, 1990). There is no longer as clearly defined a boundary between nave and sanctuary: an indication of the change in the respective competencies of priest and people. Of course, even when the dividing line between the place where liturgical actions unfold and the congregational area is no longer visible, an imaginary line may still be effectively in place, so that the congregation is not free to approach the altar or to occupy the pulpit at will. Nevertheless, it is clear that there are considerable differences in the way the relationship between sanctuary and congregational space has come to be conceived since Vatican II. In the period from Trent to Vatican II, there was an opposition between the two spaces. The sanctuary enjoyed a position of dominance over the nave: a polemical topical configuration. In most post-Vatican II churches, on the other hand, there is more of a topical configuration lying somewhere between the polemical and contractual.[13] The subjects sit or stand around a central space which is full, not empty, and which also serves as a dominating and manipulating pole. This means that the polemical-contractual configuration will on occasion lean towards the contractual

13. The analysis of the arrangement of liturgical space in G. Schiwy et al. 1976: 110-122, would be clearer if the typology of topical configurations had been used.

and on other occasions towards the polemical. It will tend towards the polemical, for example, if the priest remains at the centre, even when others are performing their liturgical tasks. Conversely, if the priest sits in the front row of the congregation and only steps up to the centre when he has some actual role to carry out, the arrangement will tend to the contractual. The location from which the priest and his assistants enter the interior is also of importance in this regard. If they enter directly from a sacristy into the sanctuary, the emphasis will be on the polemical; if they enter from a room at the back of the church, the contractual element will be more emphasized. In either instance, the respective competencies of priest and people undergo their corresponding nuancing. In feminist liturgies, the effect striven for is that of a contractual topical configuration, with the participants all sitting in a circle, which bespeaks of total equality of competencies, which are the same for all. But even here a touch of the polemical can quickly enter in when some object is placed in the middle – a candle, for instance, or a Bible – or those playing a role move into the centre, so that it is no longer empty.

I mentioned the altar as a central sender. When the altar is positioned in the middle of the central space, this is clearly an indication that the liturgy of the table is the main program.[14] If, on the other hand, the table is set a little off-centre and the ambo likewise a little off to one side, the liturgy of the word and the liturgy of the table are thereby given equal weight.

In relation to these alterations in the church building as such, it is interesting to look at the changes that have also taken place in the rituals themselves. The postconciliar marriage rite can serve as an example (Lukken 1985). The bridal couple is greeted at the door of the church by the presider, who is vested in the official liturgical dress. Right there, at the threshold of the church, two transitions are effected: from 'informal' and 'private' to 'official' and 'public' and, connected with that, from an unofficial and private being-able-to-do to a public and official being-able-to-do. After that, a spatial trajectory is traced from the church door to the altar, in the form of a solemn, ordered procession in which not only the priest and his assistants, but the bridal couple, the parents, the witnesses and others besides all take part. Non-verbally, the bridal couple is accompanied to the altar, the central focus of all official action, and installed as protagonists in the celebration to follow. By linking the bridal couple so clearly to the central symbol of official action, they themselves

14. In the celebration of the eucharist there are two main parts: the liturgy of the Word (readings) and the liturgy of the Table (the prayers and actions surrounding the eucharistic symbols of bread and wine).

are located as being competent to exercise an official role in the proceedings. As the marriage ceremony unfolds, they become the actual subjects of the performance, while the role of the priest is limited to that of coordinator (sender) of the event. He exercises his influence in inviting the couple to exchange consent and, upon completion of the performance, he ratifies (sanctions) the exchange in the name of the assembly. From this example, one can see how the changes in architectural lay-out correspond exactly to the changes in the ritual and proxemic dimensions of the rite. We have been comparing the *Rituale Romanum* of 1614 with the rites as reformed after Vatican II, and it is easy to see the conflicts that arise when people try to celebrate the reformed Roman rite of marriage in a building whose arrangements still reflect those of the era from Trent to Vatican II. There is no doubt but that such conflicts change the signification of the ritual itself.

So far, I have taken the post-Vatican II position, characterized by Muck (Muck 1988: 5) as "die Mühe um eine angemessene Verteilung der liturgischen Orte", as my starting point. Now it is Muck's opinion that, from the perspective of our culture, we have invested too much in that position. He would argue that the fixing of the spatial senders of the ritual in the interior arrangements of a church is too constraining and pleads instead for a space that rather "die Vorgänge und Darstellungsbemühingen umfasst, als dass er sie artikuliert un symbolisiert" (Muck 1988: 5; see also Schiwy *et al.* 1976: 109-113). He is against total 'fixation' of the space and argues for "handlungsoffene und bedeutungsoffene Räume mit eine offene Mitte" (Muck 1988: 2-3). Obviously, such a creative use of space would raise the question of whether the space is any longer able to govern the ritual in any fundamental way. Are there any spatial senders and even sub-senders any longer? Are specific competencies any longer tied up with various topoi? Would such an arrangement call into question the hypothesis that there is only a small number of possible topical configurations?

In my view these questions will have to be answered in the affirmative. In this connection, Darrault has a fascinating article entitled "L'espace de la thérapie" (Darrault 1984), in which he describes a highly non-verbal form of therapy which makes use of space and which has been developed in Europe over the past decade or so. This form of therapy uses a room that leaves lots of possibilities open. Needless to say, the actual structure of this space as a whole is a sender of the narrative programs that are able to unfold there. But the subjects are free to make use of that space in very creative ways. They may create spaces within the larger space. In doing so, they can determine the spatial sub-senders for themselves. It may be, for example, that when the therapist calls the child, the child goes and hides behind a pile of cushions, thereby creating a topos of inaccessibility which refuses any conjunction with the topos of the therapist. In semiotic terms, the child is trying to establish both cognitive and somatic inaccessibility. Whenever the child comes closer to the therapist, there is an imaginary boundary that is extremely important, so that, over and over again, the child moves up to this boundary and stops there, all the while making to draw back to its own space. Contact between the therapist and the child is deemed to have been made only when the child is able to cross this imaginary boundary and create one shared topos with the therapist. So it seems as though boundaries and articulated spaces, whether visible or imaginary, do influence and manipulate the programs of the subject of the performance. Still, it is possible for the subjects themselves to install the spatial sub-senders by lining up more or less opposite one another or forming a circle and so forth. In doing this, they at the same time determine the competencies attached to these topic configurations. Thus it could be said that the same spatial patterns that are found in "festgelegte Räume" crop up in "handlungsoffene Räume", but that in the latter case the subjects of the performance are themselves the architects of the space and, consequently, architects of the ritual narrative programs. So, in the end, it remains true that architecture is a fundamental and pervasive sender even of creative rituals.

At the conclusion of his study on the structure and development of the eucharistic prayer, Frank Senn notes that, despite the extensive reforms undergone by this prayer in different churches in the past twenty years, the integral celebration of the prayer itself remains relatively undeveloped (Senn 1987: 232-233). Among the elements integral to the celebration are the musical setting of the text, the accompanying visual and motor rhythms of both the presider and the community, and the architectural setting. In regard to the latter, Senn notes that little or no attention has hitherto been drawn to the fact that the quality and colour of architectural materials, the shape and height of the building, the lighting, and the way the altar is placed with respect to the congregation affect the way a congregation experiences the celebration of the eucharistic prayer. Conversely, we cannot really know what the eucharistic prayer might mean, he continues, without taking these other elements into account. But what Senn says of the eucharistic prayer is true of the liturgy as a whole. It is one of the contributions of Greimassian semiotics of architecture that it can help us determine the role of the architectural dimension in the signifying function of the liturgy as a whole.

1.   *View of the church and the pastorie from the Vierwindenlaan*

2.   *South-east wall (front) of the church and the pastorie*

3. *Main entrance to the church on the south-east side*

4. *Main church: congregational area and sanctuary*

5. Main church: congregational area, view from the sanctuary

6. Sanctuary of the main church

7.   Ceiling of the main church

8.   Devotional area

9. Baptistry

10. Pillar near the main entrance with foundation stone

11. *Portal of the south-west side entrance*

12. *South-east wall with memorial crosses*

13. *View from the main church of the chapel used for week-day services*

14. *The chapel*

15. Sanctuary of the chapel

Part II

Application

by

Mark Searle

A man walks down the street
Its a street in a strange world
Maybe it's the Third World
Maybe it's his first time around
He doesn't speak the language
He holds no currency
He is a foreign man
He is surrounded by the sound
The sound
Cattle in the marketplace
Scatterlings and orphanages
He looks around, around
He sees angels in the architecture
Spinning in infinity
He says "Amen!" and "Hallelujah!"

Paul Simon, 'You Can Call Me Al', from his album, Graceland.

CHAPTER 4
Church of SS. Peter and Paul, Tilburg:
The Exterior

The experience of Paul Simon's stranger in a strange land is a familiar one: the experience of culture shock, or total disorientation, produced by the flood of unfamiliar sights, sounds, and smells. In the midst of being overwhelmed by strange languages and usages, it comes as something of a relief to look at something as familiar and silent as buildings. For buildings, too, speak, and while it would be absurd to claim that the language of building is universal, it is true that they are usually easier to identify and thus to 'read' than the noises one hears around one in the streets, or the strange words posted in public places, or even the gestures and behaviour of an unfamiliar people. Yet while we learn to speak and are taught to read and write, it is hard to say how we are introduced to the language of architecture, how we learn to distinguish domestic from commercial buildings, for example, or schools from hospitals, or libraries from restaurants. Often we are aided by verbal or iconic signs, but the existence of such signs, even the need for such signs, does not take away from the fact that we learn to read the different places in which we find ourselves. That it happens is obvious, but for it to be able to happen there must be recognizable patterns, recurrences, redundancies, similarities and differences, which are recognizable and identifiable. There exist no dictionaries of architecture, in this sense, but out of our discursive memories we more or less successfully recognize what we see and identify it accordingly.

Moreover, while buildings may be constructed out of dead matter, of wood and stone and brick and concrete, their voice is not a dead letter. Buildings live while they remain in use: they continually speak to those who interact with them; they may find their message altered by those who refurbish them, or radically reinterpreted by those who no longer share the imaginative world of the generation that built them. Nonetheless, our buildings are silent messengers of those gods to whose service they are dedicated and whose sundry gospels are proclaimed by the "angels in the architecture spinning in infinity."

To claim that buildings 'speak' is merely to claim that they are signs. It is not implied that they were invested by their builders, or subsequently endowed by their occupants, with heavy doses of connotation, for even the most functional constructions bespeak their function, the values pursued there, the values of those who built them, and the values of those who presently occupy them. To claim that buildings speak is merely to say that, like written texts, they have a double articulation: they signify something, even if it is not easy to put one's finger immediately on all that they signify. They signify something in virtue of having a structure or form of expression and a corresponding content structure (form of the content).

The parish church of SS. Peter and Paul (*Petrus en Pauluskerk*) in the town of Tilburg in the southern Netherlands was chosen for analysis for a number of reasons. In the first place, it is a remarkably satisfying building, designed with great thoughtfulness and constructed and furnished with the closest attention to detail. At the same time, it is a most intriguing building, especially from the outside, for it offers the passer-by little clue as to its identity. It is reticent, almost taciturn in its lack of self-advertisement. What does it say, and how does it say it? Here the problems of what the outside says are quite different from those posed by the interior, so it provides an excellent example of the need to analyse the outside and inside of buildings quite separately. Moreover, the originality of the design and, in particular, the ambivalence of its exterior makes it a worthy case on which to test the strengths and limitations of the semiotic method.

We begin, then, with the outside of the building, treating it as constituting a sign-system in its own right, i.e. as being composed of two planes, that of the expression (signifier) and that of the content (signified). For the sake of the demonstration, we shall follow the method as it has been laid out in previous chapters, taking first the form of the expression and then the form of the content and proceeding step by step with each.[1]

A. THE FORM OF THE EXPRESSION

Segmentation
The site of the church is bounded by the Vierwindenlaan, which runs in an easterly arc from the north to the south of the site, by private property on the south and southwest sides, and by an access road running to the north of the church from the Vierwindenlaan to an estate of private houses and garages west of the church. The church site is fully open to the two roads, but is marked off from the private property by a high wall running from northwest to south-east, and by, first, a tall hedge along the garden of the *pastorie*, then by a two-strand wire fence along the lawn to the southeast of the church (See ground plan on cover left). The property is thus clearly delineated from neighbouring properties.

1. Ground plans of the church building are given in Appendix

1. TOPOLOGICAL CATEGORIES

The fact that buildings say something – about their purpose or identity, or about the values of their occupants – is based on the same principle, formulated by de Saussure and axiomatic ever since, that meaning is a matter of significant (i.e. signifying) differences. In looking at this church from the outside, for example, how do we know what kind of a building it is? And what does it tell us about the beliefs or values of those who built the church and worship there? Under the heading of the topological categories, we shall be systematically scouring the building and its grounds for ways in which it is 'marked' and thus rendered recognizable or intelligible. We start with the way parts of the building and its grounds are positioned in relation to each other, first on a horizontal axis, then on a vertical axis; then we look at the building's orientation, or how it directs the eye – or the access – of the visitor.

1.1. Position

1.1.1. *Horizontal*

The site has been broken up in such a way that, within the external boundaries of the property described above, further boundaries are marked off. Most important, of course, is the boundary constituted by the walls of the church itself. At the rear, this directly abuts the access road, with only enough room for a line of parking places. On the other side of the building, however, access from the road requires that one pass a thick line of shrubs, cross the parking area, go through a wall with shrubs fronting it, and traverse the courtyard before reaching the church. These differences leave little doubt as to which is the rear, and which the front of the church. The two rear doors provide direct and informal access to the interior, while the two front doors mediate much more deliberately between the inside of the church and the forecourt. Being bigger and deeper, and opening on to what can surely serve as a public gathering space, these front doors make the acts of entering or leaving more public.

And whereas entrance at the rear only means crossing a boundary as minimal as a step (and double doors), entrance at the front is distanced from the street by the series of barriers just mentioned.

The forecourt is a space enclosed by a low wall (fronted by shrubs) to form a broken trapezium which, taken with the broken trapezium that shapes the church building, serves to constitute the largest and outermost hexagon. The hexagonal motif created thereby is echoed in the honeycomb design of the courtyard paving and repeated, as we shall see, in the interior.

Signs at the entrance way in the low wall furthest from the main entrance prohibit parking in the forecourt. At the entranceway nearest the main door of the church, a bollard impedes vehicular access while permitting cyclists and pedestrians to enter. A line of bicycle racks along the inside of the low wall encourages cyclists to leave their bicycles there and to proceed on foot, together with pedestrians and those who have parked outside the wall, into the church.

1.1.2. *Vertical*

Looking at the front of the building – its 'face to the world' – we note that it is constructed on two levels, the lower being more extensive than the upper level. The lower level is represented at the front by a solid wall, broken only by the windows and doors at each extremity. The upper level, by contrast, is broken on its east and west sides by seven pairs of windows, and on the two sides to the north and the two to the south, by four pairs of windows. Each window runs almost the entire height of the wall. The walls of the upper level support a shallow-pitched hip roof culminating in two apexes, each topped with a small pinnacle.

As already noted, there is not one front entrance, but two. While they are of approximately the same size, that on the right is accentuated by being set back into the building (and thus provided with an external porch, so that arrivals are already in process of entering the building before they reach the doors). It is also accentuated by the square stained glass window of the baptistry alongside it, as opposed to the less emphatic cluster of three tall slender windows set next to the left-hand door. Moreover, within the confines of the porch, the right hand wall bears an advertisement of the times of services, while on the left hand wall a small figurative plaque at eye-level depicts the church's patrons, Peter and Paul. Thus, while there are two front entrances, it seems fair to say that the right hand door is privileged as the major entrance to the church.

The long, solid wall of the lower level, broken only by the opaque stained glass windows, is topped by an off-white aluminium trim which runs the whole length of the wall and lends emphasis to the horizontal dimension of the building. In contrast, the paired windows of the upper level, being tall and narrow, reclaim the vertical axis, only to run into the uncompromising band of white flashing which runs all the way round and is even wider than the flashing of the lower-level roof. Moreover, the shallowness of the upper roof's pitch and its double climax in two small pinnacles do little to relieve the dominant horizontality of the building. The elongated rectangular windows of the upper level seem, as we just mentioned, to represent a real upward thrust, but one which is well under the control of the horizontal vectors. Additional vertical lines are provided by two drain pipes on the front of the lower level wall and a cluster of three pipes (plus a separate narrower one) on the front edge of the main entrance, but these likewise fail to break the horizontal lines of the building. On the other hand, the fact that the upper level is smaller than the lower level does contribute to the verticality of the building, even if it is kept within the scale of the domestic buildings on surrounding sites.

The *pastorie* to the left of the courtyard is a single storey extension out of the main building and its further end is angled to fill the lower left-hand angle of the hexagon. Its public entrance faces onto the courtyard, but looks inwards towards the church rather than outward to the street. Those who would enter must first traverse the barriers (two lines of shrubbery, the second backed by a wall) which intervene between the church and the public street, and cross the courtyard. The *pastorie*, in contrast to the church (at least at ground level) and the reception complex, has several windows looking out onto the courtyard and the public lawn. They are of a normal domestic size. The doorway, too, is much like the doorways of private houses in the neighbourhood. Thus, the *pastorie* is distinguished from the rest of the complex by its domestic scale. Though the whole edifice is nowhere taller than the surrounding private residences, the *pastorie* is the only section which also has windows and a doorway on a domestic scale.

It should also be noted that the space between the *pastorie* and the neighbouring private residence is screened off from the view both of the neighbours and of visitors to the church by a tall (2m.) hedge, creating a *hortus conclusus* belonging to the *pastorie* and accessible only via equally tall barred gates or from the *pastorie* itself. It should also be added that the gates do not offer even visual access to the garden: one because of its position at the side of the *pastorie*, the other because some solid covering has been affixed to the gate to block the view.

At the other end of the building from the *pastorie*, the reception rooms adjoin the courtyard but have no windows onto the courtyard and no external access. Access is through the main entrance to the church (A), or through the rear entrance (D). The windows of the reception area are taller than appears customary in local domestic architecture, being more reminiscent of business premises. Like the windows of the *pastorie*, and like all domestic windows in the area, they are decked with net curtains. The toilet and cloakroom areas being closest to the front door of the church, the windows on the outside wall of that end of the reception complex are small and high. The windows along the rear wall of the building are equally small and high, admitting light but not giving any view of the interior (sacristies). The windows of the weekday chapel (*dagkapel*) match the larger windows of the reception area (*receptieruimte*), even to number (five), size, and style of curtain.

In summary, this is a building in which horizontal lines dominate over the vertical, the front is more imposing than the rear, and the right side is more imposing than the left. Despite its size, which seems to suggest it is not used, at least in its entirety, as a private residence, the domestic scale dominates over the public. We might also say that the human wins out over the super-human, for it is a building that seems careful to accommodate itself to the human scale and refuses to use its size to overawe the visitor.

1.1.2. Orientation

The design of the building (with its four entrances at east, west, north and south) and its surrounds (especially the two main pathways leading from the Vierwindenlaan to the courtyard) is such as to create a movement of convergence among those arriving and of divergence among those departing. Note that, unlike many buildings, it is designed to accommodate the arrival and departure of large numbers of people more or less *simultaneously*, and that it lays out pathways which turn arriving into convergence and departing into divergence. In part this is the effect of aligning the building with the only 45 degree angle of the site, and facing its front towards its broadest boundary, the road. Two broad pathways lead from the road to the courtyard. For the first few meters, they are accessible to motor vehicles and cycles, as well as pedestrians. Vehicles turn aside, however, into the parking lanes, leaving the path to pedestrians and cyclists. Cyclists dismount and park their machines just inside the low outer wall of the courtyard, so that finally it is only pedestrians who converge on the two entrances.

The angling of the main entrance, forming a porch and creating a sense of already entering the building before the door has been reached, 'funnels' arrivals into the interior. Arrivals using the other door are similarly funneled between the long closed wall of the church and the bent arm of the *pastorie*. The same is true, on a lesser scale at the back of the church where the two rear entrances – each, like the front entrances, equipped with a double set of inner and outer doors – are set back into the building and raised at least one step above the ground.

To return to the front courtyard. While it is well-defined by the low walls along its front and right sides, by the solid wall of the church along its back side, and by the *pastorie* at its left, it is nonetheless a wide, open space, accessible by generously wide paths. It is centred by a tall, three-globe lamp surrounded by a bed of shrubbery. At night, this lamp illuminates the whole courtyard sufficiently for visitors to the church to find their way in and out with ease. Thus the courtyard is both a transition space and a space for brief, informal gatherings before or after the services. As the terminus of the two main pathways, it is marked by the oppositions /broad/ vs /narrow/ and /free/ vs /directed/. Visitors, having been led by the path to this point now have to decide which entrance to opt for: the main entrance on the right or the secondary entrance on the left. The primacy of one entrance over the other is indicated only very subtly, as we saw above.

Thus the orientation of the front of the building seems to be one of required convergence, followed by a permit to diverge, followed (inside) by a resumption of the movement of convergence.

As we have seen, there are four entrances, but those giving on to the front courtyard are larger than those at the back, while that on the east corner of the building is slightly larger and more receptive than that on the south and is clearly the one which would be used for solemn entrances, as in marriages and funerals.

2. PLASTIC CATEGORIES

Having examined how the different parts of the property are related to each other, we will now look at how the building speaks through the use of different-coloured materials and the employment of recurring shapes.

2.1. Chromatic Categories

The whole building is constructed of variegated (predominantly sand-coloured) brick. All the surrounding private dwellings are also of brick, mostly of a reddish hue, though the house to the west and its surrounding wall are painted white. Nevertheless, the overall effect is that of a building that merges into the neighbourhood in virtue of the materials used, rather than one that stands out.

The only architectural relief to the light brickwork is provided by the off-white of the flashing running along the top edge of the walls of the church (upper and lower levels) and *pastorie*, by the translucent windows of the upper level of the church, by the white-curtained windows of the *pastorie*, by the wooden framework of the glass doors, and by the dark rectangular shapes of the stained glass windows at each end of the front wall of the church. The straight lines and sharp angles of the building are somewhat softened by the lawns to east and north, the shrubbery lining each side of the parking area and masking the low walls, and the shrubs around the lamp at the center of the courtyard. There are also roses growing against the long front wall of the church. Three birch trees are growing on the north lawn and one on the east lawn, in the narrow angle between the east path and the front drive of the adjoining house. The street itself is lined with mapletrees. Most of the shrubs are low evergreens and are allowed to grow naturally, but the hedge separating the private garden of the *pastorie* from the east lawn is deciduous and is clipped straight and square. Again, the white curtained windows, the natural wood window frames, the decidious trees and evergreen shrubs, are all very common in the neighbourhood. Only the dark shapes of the stained-glass windows seem distinctive, chromatically.

The two pathways are paved with grey concrete tiles, as are the sidewalk along the Vierwindenlaan and the access road running behind the church. The parking spaces, located on four sides of the church, are paved with red and yellow brick. The courtyard is paved with hexagonal concrete tiles, with lighter (sand-coloured) tiles creating a honeycomb pattern of larger hexagons. While the scale of the property and especially the provision of parking places marks the church off from the neighborhood, the use of brick or patterned tile for outside paving is typical of the area.

2.2. Eidetics

The shapes presented to the visitor by the exterior of the church are all oblongs: the horizontal oblongs of the front wall of the church, the *pastorie*, and the reception rooms. Vertical oblongs are represented by the windows in the upper level of the church, by the stained glass windows to the left on the lower level, by the tall windows in the reception complex, and by the more standard in the *pastorie*. The only true square is that of the baptistry window, though the three narrow oblong windows at the other end also form a square and the doorways are close to being squares.

In contrast to all these right angles, the roof, seen from the front of the church, is trapeze-shaped, while the 60-degree angle of the *pastorie* and that of the low wall facing the church echo the angles of the hexagons patterning the courtyard. What can be seen of the upper level of the church from the ground suggests that it, too, is hexagonal. It is only when seen from above, however, or from the plans, that the dominance of the hexagon becomes apparent: it is not only the pattern of the courtyard paving, but the outer shape of the whole complex of church-*pastorie*-courtyard-reception rooms. Thus, while a two-dimensional hexagonal pattern is there to be seen on the ground of the forecourt, a three-dimensional hexagon formed by the back and sides of the church and the low wall running round the courtyard is already enclosing the visitor (See ground plan 1).

It might also be worth noting that, in contrast to the perfect hexagons of the paving stones, the hexagonal outline of the building and forecourt is broken by the rear entrances to the church and by the openings through which the visitor passes from the pathways to the courtyard. More strikingly, the hexagon's upper and lower halves are out of alignment on the north and south sides. The garage door of the *pastorie* and the solid end-wall of the reception rooms break the symmetry of the hexagonal form. The two-dimensional hexagons are perfect: the three-dimensional hexagon is broken.

B. THE FORM OF THE CONTENT

In describing the building as we have done, we have been trying to identify the patterns of similarity and difference which constitute the 'language' of the building. Now we try to work out what the building is saying, inevitably drawing, as all interpretation must, on a certain 'discoursive memory' which enables us to recognize patterns of difference or of similarity from a lifetime of experience with other buildings. Note that we are speaking of *patterns* here, rather than of single elements. A building, we have stressed, is a 'semi-symbolic system', where the relationship of signification obtains, not between individual elements of the expression (signifier) and individual elements of the content (signified), but between sets of relationships between elements on one plane and sets of relationships between elements on the other plane .(See Ch.2.1, above).

1. THE LEVEL OF DISCOURSIVE STRUCTURES

1.1. Discoursive Syntax

1.1.1. *Actorialization*

The building bears no traces of the instance of enunciation: neither enunciator nor enunciatee is mentioned anywhere. Whereas it is not uncommon for churches and other buildings to have a foundation stone or memorial tablet visible from the outside and engraved with the names of those who commissioned the building, or paid for it, or with some sort of dedication, nothing of the kind is found here: there is no inscription of the dedication of the church or of the identity of its users.

On the other hand, the plaque announcing the *'Pastorie'* could be read as
an implicit reference to the *pastor* as recipient – *destinataire* – of the
building, by analogy with 'old people's home' or *ziekenhuis*.[2]

1.1.2. *Temporalization*

There are no temporal disengagements of the enunciation on the outside
of the church: no date for the foundation laying, or for the opening or the
consecration. Times of Masses posted in the main entrance represent
temporal programming only loosely associated with the temporal disengagement of the building itself.

1.1.3. *Spatialization*

Given that a building is a kind of utterance, and one that is manifested
primarily in spatial terms, the spatial organization of the building-as-dis-
course is clearly of primary importance. Here we shall examine the way
the building is projected first in terms of spatial localization and then in
terms of spatial programming.

1.1.3.1. *Spatial localization*
Spatial localization refers to the way the construction is organized in
space, particularly as it differentiates itself from surrounding spaces. This
distinction between a space and its surrounding spaces is the distinction
between topic and heterotopic spaces ('here' vs 'elsewhere'). But such a
distinction is obviously entirely relative, depending on where one stands.
Nonetheless, a certain hierarchy can be identified: in opposition to the
church site, the surrounding residential area is heterotopic; in relation to
the interior of the church, the exterior forecourt and the surrounding
lawns and parking areas are heterotopic.

1.1.3.2. *Spatial Programming*
How does the building's relationship to its surroundings, especially to the
street(s), program the behaviour of those who enter or leave?

First, we need to distinguish between front and back entrances. Whereas
rear doors are usually more or less functional, front entranceways speak
of a building's relation to the world. For example, they are likely to have
a more pronounced transitional character than do rear entrances. Rear

---

2. The text reads: PASTORIE *pastorale* SS. PETRUS EN PAULUS; roughly, 'House of the
Pastor *Pastoral Ministry* Sts. Peter and Paul'. 'Ziekenhuis' (lit. 'house for the sick'), is a
hospital.

2007

Mark Torgersen
A All of Tun.
NA 4600.T67
2007

doors do not usually make a statement about what it means to enter this house, and those who use the rear doors do not usually share or assume the values associated with, and mediated by, the front entrance. Thus, tradesmen may be sent to the backdoor, but it would be an insult to a guest to be sent to the back door and an affront to the family for a visitor to enter unannounced through the back. At a hospital, patients are not generally admitted through the delivery entrance. Similarly, it would be unthinkable for a bridal party or a funeral cortege – under normal circumstances – to enter the church through any but the main door. Thus the back and sides of the building can be regarded as 'insignificant', becoming significant only – and precisely – when their 'insignificance' is itself significant.

If we focus, then, on the front, or courtyard side of SS. Peter and Paul, we are struck by the rather elaborate approach to the church from the Vierwindenlaan. Cars may enter either from the access road to the north (turning left immediately to enter the carpark at the side of the church rather than going on to the parking spots behind the church), or directly from the street in the south. Pedestrians and cyclists may use either of these entrances, but they also have an additional pathway leading directly from the Vierwindenlaan into the courtyard. But note the succession of boundaries that have to be crossed. All comers, whatever their mode of travel, pass the first line of shrubs and enter upon church property. They are on site, but not yet in the courtyard. Access to the courtyard is through one of two broad gates in the low wall running around the south east and south west sides of the court. Both entrances are wide enough to admit cars if needs be, but one bears a written prohibition against vehicular access, while the other entrance is blocked to cars by a bollard. This means that, in practice, no cars enter the courtyard unless it be to bring handicapped people to the main door. Hearses and wedding limousines drive in through the southernmost entrance and, the bollard being removed for the occasion, drive out to the north.

Once in the courtyard, the visitor is faced by the long solid southwest wall of the church itself and by a choice of two entrances. Though one of these is slightly more of an entrance than the other, one wonders about this duplication. There are two entrances to the courtyard, two front entrances to the church and two rear entrances. Inside, there are two entrances to the baptistry. There are also two entrances to the reception area, from (1) and (17), and two entrances – via (11) – to the church from the sacristies, and two ways of entering the church from each sacristy: either through (11), or through (4). It is as if there was a reluctance to define a single main door or central aisle as a focus for passing in and out. Instead of coming together at a single entrance, people enter from all directions and only come together once they are inside. Thus there is a sense of very gradual convergence: from street, to parking lot, to court- yard, to one or other entranceway, and so into the interior of the build- ing. With the entrances situated at the corners, and with the 'main door' not really proclaiming itself very loudly as such, it is hard to say whether the act of entering is devalued or simply reinterpreted.

1.1.3.3. Spatial aspectualization

Spatial aspectualization corresponds to what an observer might notice about a subject's relationship to the spatial environment insofar as this af- fects the subject's ability to move or to see across spaces. In analysing a given space (either a natural or a constructed space), the presence of a hy- pothetical actor is postulated, in regard to whom the relationship be- tween spaces, or objects in space, can be evaluated as near or far, easily accessible or unattainable, and so forth. Similarly in terms of visibility: what is visible and what is not from the vantagepoint of the hypothetical subject?

Situated on a bend in the road, the church of SS. Peter and Paul is a pro- minent but not dominant feature of the neighborhood. Traffic heading northwards, especially, can hardly fail to see it. Though the church is set back from the road, it is not hidden. People driving in the opposite direc- tion are less likely to notice it, since the first view is of the *receptieruimte*, and even this is partly screened by the trees on the north lawn. The next view is across the courtyard to the *pastorie*. As we have already re- marked, both the reception area and the priest's residence are domestic in appearance and unlikely to catch the eye. To see the church itself, anyone passing by in a car would have to turn their head rather deliberately. In neither direction is any clear indication given that this is a church.

For anyone who stops to look at the building, the exterior of SS. Peter and Paul's is somewhat unwelcoming. Vehicular access to the church is possible only by means of two widely separated pathways and the access road running along the back of the property. The church and its fore- court are set well back from the street and fenced off by two lines of bar- ricades, first the shrubbery running along the sidewalk, then the wall and shrubbery separating the courtyard from the parking spaces. Once the forecourt has been reached, the hypothetical visitor must choose by which door to enter with little clue given as to which has priority.

Visually, the church is open to the world in that the walls and shrubbery are kept low to permit a full view of the church. On the other hand, the construction of the church itself presents the view of a solid wall. Neither the windows of the upper level nor the glass doors of the lower level offer any view of the interior. Nor are there any signs, written or iconic, to indicate the nature of the building to an observer standing at the edge of the property. Such verbal notices as there are – the nameplate on the *pastorie*, the noticeboards in the porch of the *pastorie* and in the porch at the main entrance to the church – can only be read from close up. In the main entranceway, there is a blue ceramic plaque representing the apostles Peter and Paul mounted on the wall to the left, but this is likewise not identifiable from a distance of more than a few meters. The left-hand front entrance and the two rear entrances have no indication whatsoever of what it is to which they offer access. The windows of the sacristies are well above eye-level, while those of the *receptieruimte* and the weekday chapel are covered with sheer curtains. The doors are of glass, but none of them gives a direct view into the interior and, except at night when the interior lights are on, it is almost impossible to see across the hallway to the second set of doors. (Indeed, the inside doors of the main entrance are of frosted glass.)

Thus, while the low lines of the walls and shrubbery in front of the building seem to expose the church to the view of the passer-by, no visual access is given to the interior and few external clues are given as to the nature of the building. Similarly, physical access, while not difficult, is nonetheless restricted, and certainly not invited.

1.2. Discoursive Semantics

Under this heading we wish to identify the figurativizations in virtue of which this building 'speaks' and is recognizable as similar to, or representative of, recognizable kinds of building. What architectural 'micro-narratives' are evoked by this building's exterior? What figurative trajectories does it employ? These can best be identified by comparing this building with other buildings or types of buildings, drawing on the 'discoursive memory'. In the following table, we can see at once the features that this church has with domestic buildings, public buildings, and traditional churches in this part of the Netherlands.

Domestic Buildings	Public Buildings	Tradit.Church
Height of building	Size of exterior doors	
	Glass doors	
	Swing doors	
size of windows		stained glass
windows looking out		
curtains	curtains	

porcelain plaque
at main door
street number by door

	car parking	parking
	forecourt	forecourt
shrubs, flowers	shrubs, flowers	

FIGURE 11

Conversely, this building lacks the tower or steeple and bells associated with traditional churches, just as it lacks an imposing front entrance or any exterior crucifix or statues such as are characteristic of Catholic churches in this part of the world.

The building has too many features in common with public buildings to be taken for a private residence; yet it has too many features of a private residence for the casual observer to identify it at once as a public building or a church. If we ask what the building looks like, we need to make an immediate distinction. The left-hand section of the building (*pastorie*) looks from the street like a private house, whereas the rest of the building is hard to identify.

Focussing on the rest of the building, the visitor notes its size, the large number of parking places, the breadth of the doors, all of which suggest that this building is designed with patterns of behaviour in mind which will bring together relatively large numbers of people at the same time. The outside of the building gives little clue to the arrangement of the inner space, but the lack of windows on the first floor suggests that it might not be broken up into separate rooms, and the windows of the upper level, appearing to open onto a large interior space, confirms the impression that this is a place of assembly.

Does the building give clues as to its purpose? It does not, and this fact itself immediately rules out a number of possible functions. For example, a theater would identify itself by name and would have display cases on the street advertising its current and future productions. It could be an auction room, a public library, a swimming pool, a masonic temple, or a synagogue. It is too large to be a domestic residence, too short of windows to be an office complex or a school, too discreet to be a commercial enterprise. It does not invite visitors, nor does it exclude them. It does not advertise for clients or invite attendance. It is not the kind of building where people might wander in off the street by accident. For all its size, it remains a very private building.

Does its architectural style suggest any sort of iconicity or imitation?

Does it set out to resemble something other than itself, or adopt a recognizable style? There is something tent-like about the scale of the central section and the shape of the roof, whose two pinnacles could be the main poles of the 'big top'. If anything, though, the shape of the pinnacles is reminiscent of those seen on the roof-ends of Dutch farmhouses. (There is such a farm house, its lands all now thoroughly urbanized, at the corner of the Bredaseweg and the Academielaan, just a hundred meters from the church!)

In sum, the only thing that an external observer can say about it with any degree of confidence is that it is a place of assembly. The fact that it is busy only for an hour on Saturday evenings and for a couple of hours on Sunday mornings confirms that it is a church. So does the fact of having a private residence in such close proximity to a public building: theater directors, auctioneers and swimming-pool managers do not usually live at their place of employment, whereas clergy commonly do.

Thus the building seems to feature the following figurative values. It is 'organizational' rather than 'domestic' in character; admission is for 'membership only' rather than open to the 'general public'; it tends towards the 'anonymous' rather than the 'identifiable'; it is a building that is 'reticent' rather than 'self-advertizing', and characterized by 'secrecy' rather than 'publicity'. On the other hand, the fact that it is a place of assembly, with a private residence attached, (plus, perhaps, the stained glass windows, though these are difficult to identify from the outside), suggests that its purpose is 'religious' rather than 'secular', while the lack of any apparent felt need to advertize itself or to proselytize perhaps suggests a religious affiliation that is 'mainline' rather than 'sectarian'.

Traditional Dutch churches rarely identify themselves with name-displays or signs (as is usual in the US and UK), perhaps because:
  a. their architecture identifies them unmistakably as churches;
  b. certain iconic figures (e.g. statue of the Sacred Heart) or the absence thereof usually identify them as Catholic or Reformed;
  c. they are usually in immediate juxtaposition to some public space: square, crossroads, etc.
  d. their size and position and lack of verbal identification speak of the assumption that everyone knows what they are.

This church, however, lacks the usual figurative identification which makes a church 'look like a church'. It doesn't look like a church; it does not identify itself in natural language as being a church; it doesn't adjoin a public site, such as a market place or a main street.

The 'privacy' of this building is figurativized in part by the windowless walls (wall of church, end wall of reception area) which represent a closed 'face to the world', and in part by the distance that has to be traversed in passing from 'outside' to 'inside'. (Cfr. narrative syntax, below). Its 'organizational' character, in contrast to the 'domestic' character of the other buildings in the neighborhood, is indicated by its scale, the number of parking places, the size of its entryways, and the large forecourt. The lack of any self-advertisement suggests that it is open to 'members only', as opposed to the 'general public', that is 'reticent', 'anonymous' and 'secretive'. On the other hand, the patterns of use, especially at weekends, indicate that it is indeed a church: that it is a 'religious' building open on Sundays, rather than a 'secular' building, like the schools on the nearby Schout Crillaertstraat, which are open only during the week. But, if it is religious, it is discreetly so: it does not assert its organizational identity or show any attempt at proselytizing. In that sense, it appears – in Troeltch's terminology – more the building of a church than of a sect. But is the lack of any outward identifying sign – such as a name or, more likely, a cross – an indication of the community's self-assurance about the church's role in the neighborhood, so that any identifying sign would be superfluous, or is it indicative of a mentality which prefers for whatever reason to keep a low profile?

2. THE SURFACE LEVEL

The visitor to SS. Peter and Paul is confronted with the task of making the transition from street to church. The successful completion of this task requires in turn certain competencies which are acquired through conjunction with a series of different *topoi*.

2.1. The Street and the Forecourt

Here the narrative program (NP) 'travelling' comes to an end and is succeeded by the NP 'gathering'.

The lay-out of the church grounds and their relationship to the street constitute a series of manipulations of virtual (potential) Subjects of the NP of 'gathering' and at the same time invest those Subjects with various competencies to make them actual Subjects of the performance.

To take manipulation first, we might say that the physical barriers established by the brick walls, the shrubbery, and the bollard constitute a negative manipulation: a having-not-to-do. Conversely, the driveways from the road to the parking lots represent a negation of that prohibition (a not-having-not-to-do) by giving permission for vehicular and pedestrian traffic to enter. On the other hand, the signs at one entrance to the forecourt and the bollard at the other represent a selective prohibition 'having-not-to-drive' and 'having-to-walk' – selective because it does not apply to cyclists. At the same time, these openings constitute a manipulation in the form of permission to proceed further, a permission granted only to pedestrians and cyclists.

The parking spots on the street and on the church property are Objects of value which provide modal competencies of 'pouvoir-faire' (being able to park and to leave one's car) and 'vouloir-faire' (being willing to proceed on foot). Bicycle racks serve the same function for cyclists. Thus the parking spots, the bicycle racks, the signs, the brick-wall-and-shrubbery barriers, all cooperate in the modalization of the subjects of the NP of 'gathering', both negatively (preventing car and bicycles entering the church) and positively (providing parking places and inviting drivers and passengers and, within the courtyard, cyclists, to proceed on foot.

Note that the subject of the NP 'gathering' is collective. More precisely, the individual subjects, in carrying out these modalizing performances are already divesting themselves of their individuating characteristics (cars, bicycles) and adopting a common thematic role (pedestrian). The forecourt *requires* that, however people may have arrived, they all enter on foot, even if only for the last few yards.

Note also that the passer-by is enabled to see the building, even though it is set well back off the street, because the barriers that mark it off from the street (bushes, walls) are kept low. Nevertheless, the building gives little clue to its identity at this distance.

2.2. Forecourt and Building

The visitor standing in the middle of the forecourt faces a long blank wall with a door at each end, but little or no clue as to which entrance to take. Such a visitor is modalized as follows.

The wall prevents physical access (making-not-able-to-do) and also has the effect of discouraging visitors from seeking access (making-not-to-want-to-do). On the other hand, the existence of the doors is inviting (making-to-want-to-do), while leaving the visitor free to choose either entrance (not-having-to-do).

For their part, the doors on the front side of the building (unlike those on the back) are wide enough to be able to offer access to several people at once, which suggests that the performance for which the building is designed may be one that has a collective actant or, at least, a large number of individual actants. These doors, moreover, are made of glass and serve as a significant source of natural light inside the building, but the fact that they open onto a rather small lobby or hallway and are then followed by another set of glass doors means that the outsider peering in actually sees little or nothing of the interior. Even with the interior lights on, the doors are so angled that they avoid giving any direct view of what is inside.

In short, then, the doors and the walls collaborate in manipulating or virtualizing a Subject by forbidding direct access, whether physical or visual, to the interior and, at the same time encouraging the use of the limited access that is provided. They also actualize the Subject, by endowing it with various competencies, both pragmatic (being-able-to-enter) and cognitive (being-able-to-see-or-recognize). The overall effect is that of a near-complete separation of the interior space and its activities from the outside world. It is as if the Sender had issued a double mandate: to the 'world', a having-not-to-enter; to the 'church', a having-not-to-overflow-to-the-outside.

2.3. Forecourt and Pastorie

Once in the forecourt, the *pastorie* is an option, but it is differentiated from the rest of the building by its domestic scale and its multiple windows. All these windows, however, are covered with gauze curtains. They let light in, but to the outside they represent the modal values of not-being-able-to-enter and not-being-able-to-see-the-interior. The semantic value conveyed by the curtained windows is therefore that of 'privacy'.

The doorway and its (curtained) glass door permit entrance under certain conditions, mainly the cooperation of those inside. A sign beside the door indicates the nature of the building (*pastorie*, or presbytery) and list several names. It thus provides those who read it with the *savoir* necessary for any number of unspecified NPs. The doorbell, on the other hand, is a modal object which makes the visitor competent to act as a Sender and to summon the occupant(s) to open the door, a performance necessary to most of the other main performances which one might associate with doorways. In contrast, the doors of the church have no door bell and the visitor is able to enter only in virtue of an unknown Sender who has invited and permitted entry by opening the doors ahead of time.

To highlight these contrasts, we can set out the opposing semantic values on the semiotic square on the opposite page (figure 12).

Meaning is a matter of differences. Here we have one example – that of the doors and gates in the forecourt – which illustrates how a 'system' of

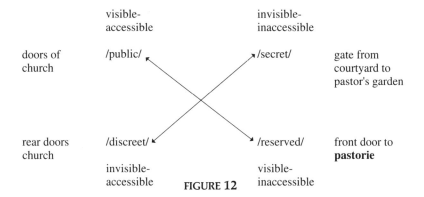

FIGURE 12

differences (whether doors can be seen through or not, whether they are open or locked) provides a language through which things speak. Note, however, that the system is semi-symbolic, not symbolic: the correspondence is not between units on the plane of signification and units on the plane of content, but between a series or pattern of signifying units and a corresponding pattern of meanings. A single door, devoid of context or not part of a system, has no meaning.

3. THE DEEP LEVEL

Here we are trying to identify the axiological values that govern the specific kind of meaning projected by the exterior of this building. We can move towards this by recalling what we have been able to establish in our analysis so far.

First, the exterior does not proclaim, as many buildings do, the identity of the building, its purpose, or the identity of the owners or users.

Second, the exterior is open to view (it is not hidden behind a high wall), but it allows no glimpse of the interior and does not encourage casual visitors to enter and discover for themselves.

Third, its scale, the size of its doors, the provision of extensive parking space, and the suggestion given by the second storey windows of a large open space inside, all add up to identify this as a public building. Yet its public character is muted by the lack of guidance given to visitors, so we might better describe it as a semi-public building: one open to members, rather than to the general public. Moreover, its public character is further modified by the low vertical lines, the low walls and banks of shrubbery, all of which suggest a desire to respect the residential character of the neighborhood, to fit in rather than to stand out.

Fourth, it is identifiable as a church only in virtue of the small notice-board with times of Masses which is found on the wall of the main entrance, and by the patterns of use (mainly Sunday mornings). But, given it is a church, it is in striking contrast with other churches in the city of Tilburg. Whereas they, almost without exception, are large imposing buildings, dominating their surroundings, SS. Peter and Paul is very much built to human scale, no taller than any of the nearby houses. Whereas the traditional churches are erected in public places like squares and thoroughfares, and make their presence felt on the general public, SS. Peter and Paul is nestled discreetly in a quiet residential area and set well back from the road. Whereas the other churches use height and size to testify to the power and transcendence of God and his church, SS. Peter and Paul is discreet, anonymous and apparently content to assume the domestic values of a relatively affluent neighborhood. Thus, while being a church, the *Petrus en Pauluskerk* opts not to identify itself with the traditional church and defines its relationship to the larger world quite differently. It is as if the exterior issues a double mandate: to the world, a discouragement against entering; to the church within, a prohibition against overflowing into secular life around it. It no longer jostles with the world on the sidewalks and in the market-place, but maintains its reserve and keeps its distance.

It might be tempting to describe this church as marked by ambiguity, but ambiguity is defined as 'the property of utterances which simultaneously presents several possible readings or interpretations, with no single one dominating over the other' (Greimas/Courtés 1979: s.v. Ambiguité). The problem confronting the visitor to SS. Peter and Paul, however, is not that one cannot finally choose between several possible interpretations of the identity of the building, but that that identity is not readily recognized. The visitor has to undertake a process of veridiction, searching for clues as to what sort of a place it is and only finally, by the sort of process of elimination we have conducted here, coming to recognize that it must be a church. It does not seem that the exterior of SS. Peter and Paul is ambiguous, therefore, but merely secretive. The problem is one of veridiction, of establishing the relationship between what the building seems to be and what it really is. The various veridictory categories can be set out on the semiotic square on the opposite page (Greimas/Courtés 1979: s.v. Véridictoires (modalités -)) (figure 13).

In the final analysis, it is this tension between being and not seeming which seems best to account for the conflicting values we have identified in our analysis.

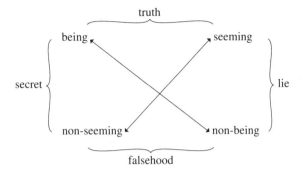

FIGURE 13

C. CONCLUSION

It is tempting to speculate on why this Roman Catholic parish church should be so secretive, so reticent to identify itself for what it is. Planned in the late sixties and built in the early seventies, this building went up during a time of profound transition for Dutch Catholicism. Was it simply an honest effort to translate into bricks and mortar the new, less triumphalist ecclesiology of the church as the People of God? Or did it represent, however unconsciously, a certain failure of nerve before the wave of secularization that swept over Dutch society in the sixties? It is for historians, rather than semioticians, to answer such questions by hunting for clues as to the mind of those involved at the time. What this analysis is intended to demonstrate is how the exterior of a building presents itself to be read by those who encounter it, how the form of the expression is articulated with the form of the content to make such a reading possible. As is the case with written texts, not every reader will take the time to undertake a really close reading, but will skim the signifying object more or less unthinkingly and 'make sense' of it. Nonetheless, whatever the reader may make of it, however the viewer may react to it, the building is there, awaiting our attention.

Chapter 5
Church of SS. Peter and Paul, Tilburg:
The Interior

The interior arrangement, furnishing and decoration of any building provides copious information about the kinds of transactions which occur there and about the values of those who occupy the space. Reading such information implies viewing the building and its arrangement as a complex sign, consisting of a signifying syntagm (the form of the expression) and a signified syntagm (the form of the content).

This is what Felix Thürlemann calls the plastic level and the figurative level respectively. The 'plastic level' is that of the architectonic qualities of the building, regardless of any representational function they may serve; the 'figurative level' is the building insofar as it refers to something other than itself, i.e. insofar as it 'presents' itself as intelligible to its visitors and insofar as it 'represents' allusions to other times, places or buildings, or simply an 'image' of the values of those responsible for it.

Here we begin by looking at the form of the expression or the plastic level, seeing how the space is divided up and the kinds of oppositions which are thereby created. But whereas Thürlemann, working with paintings, begins with chromatics to identify the different units or 'elements', as he calls them, of the expression, in the analysis of built space it is best to begin with the topological categories of position and orientation and then move to the plastic categories, both chromatic and eidetic. At the risk of a certain amount of repetition, this enables us to account for the appearance of the different spaces, their relationship to each other and the way in which continuities and discontinuities are registered.

A. THE FORM OF THE EXPRESSION

'Plastic' or visual semiotics has developed four categories of elements which can be used to segment the architectural 'text' and to establish the basic units of expression: two topological (position and orientation) and two plastic (chromatics and eidetics).

1. TOPOLOGICAL CATEGORIES

1.1 Position

1.1.1. The interior of the building is a contained or bounded space which is further subdivided into component spaces. The first task is to identify those subspaces and to situate them within the configurations they form with each other.

1.1.2. *The vertical axis*

Areas (9) and (10) are twice as high as the rest of the building and have a pitched ceiling whereas all other areas have a flat ceiling. The lower level of (9) is approximately the same height as that of the adjacent space (4) and consists of square or vertical oblong openings between square brick pillars, to create an 'open wall', except on the side behind (10) where a solid wall divides (9) from areas (11) to (14). The upper level, marked off by the white lintels spanning the pillars and by the corbels carrying the roof supports, is a clerestory of tall narrow windows grouped in pairs (seven pairs on the long east and west sides, four on each of the shorter sides). This provides the biggest single infusion of natural light into the building. The lower wall, then, is broken to admit large numbers of people, while the upper level wall is broken to admit large amounts of daylight.

The baptistry (8), in contrast, has the same level ceiling as the rest of the building, but its floor is two steps below the floor-level of the rest.

The sanctuary (10) is raised one step above the floor of (9), while the pre-siders' chairs are rised a further step. The altar in (6), too, stands on a platform one step above ground level, but has no further elevation for a presider's chair.

1.1.1.3 *The horizontal axis*
The single largest space in the interior of the building is (9). It forms a slightly elongated hexagon and contains another hexagon (10) embedded in it. These two spaces form a configuration we shall refer to henceforth as 'the main church'. The baptistry is also hexagonal, whereas, with few exceptions to be noted later, the other spaces are all rectangular. This already suggests a certain distinctiveness for these three areas: (9), (10), and (8).

The main church is, as noted, a slightly elongated hexagon, marked off from the transition space (4) that surrounds it on five sides by the brick pillars and on the sixth side by a wall. The boundaries of the area (9) are further marked by a broad band of black vinyl flooring running between the pillars and by the back row of chairs providing the seating in (9). The fact that icons are mounted on both sides of the pillars that mark the boundary between (9) and (4) suggests a particular value attached to this boundary. The wall separating the main church from the sacristies is solid save for the passageway (11) to the sacristies. This passageway is concealed from the view of the congregation by a freestanding wall which, besides concealing the entrance to the sacristies, serves to move the sanctuary (10) out into the main church. (10) remains both embedded and peripheral, but the free-standing wall accentuates the embeddedness and plays down the peripheral character of (10).

The *dagkapel* and the *receptieruimte* share a number of features in common. They are both oblong spaces ending in an irregular hexagon. Both have identical numbers and kinds of windows to the outside. Both are so juxtaposed to the main church as to create with it a trapeze and themselves to converge in a northwesterly direction. They differ, however, in that the reception rooms are completely cut off from the church by a solid wall, so that it is only possible to pass from one to the other by going through the external entranceways (1) and (17). The weekday chapel, on the other hand, is fully open to the main interior space of the church and is only demarcated from (4) by four slender round pillars.

The weekday chapel and the reception area thus flank the main church, but they are not quite equal. Unlike the *dagkapel*, the reception complex (19-26) is not only inaccessible from the church but lies *outside* the trapeze it forms with the *dagkapel*, while the *dagkapel* is *within* the trapeze. Even though the weekday chapel is twinned with the reception area, therefore, it differs from it by being in physical continuity with the main church, the sacristies, the devotional space and the baptistry.

The *devotieruimte* (7) and the baptistry (8) occupy analogous positions as sub-areas of the main church, both located on the south-east wall adjacent to the main entrance and the second entrance respectively.

The *devotieruimte* is an open corner with four angles, an incomplete hexagon. Its walls screen it from the entranceway (B) and the related area of (4), but it is entirely open and accessible to passers-by. In the outer wall, adjacent to the *devotieruimte*, are three stained glass windows of highly stylized, almost abstract design.

The *baptistry*, in contrast, while similarly screened from the nearby entranceway, is a perfect hexagon. The fact that the hexagon is com-

pleted only by a low wall and the steps means that it is fully visible to all
leaving (9). Its boundaries with the transition area (4) and hence with the
rest of the interior of the church is marked by the wall and steps, as mentioned, and by two slender metal pillars (identical with those which bound
the *dagkapel*) in the angles of the hexagon. The low wall runs between the
pillars and contains a flowerbed, while a set of steps separates the wall
from the exterior wall at each of its ends. There is a square stained glass
window in the outer wall with a schematic or semi-abstract design of
baptismal motifs: a dove (or phoenix?), flowing water, a fountain, a sun.
At the center of the baptistery stands an hexagonal font, attended by a
paschal candle.

The sacristies (12-13) and (14) occupy symmetrical positions in relation to
the main church area (9-10). Neither opens directly onto either (9) or (10).
From (10), the entrance to each via (11) is screened by the free-standing
wall. From (9), the entrances to (13) and (14) from (4) are screened by the
pillars which demarcate the congregational space and support the upper
level walls.

The area (4) is a transition space which serves both to separate and to link
the main church with the other spaces in the church and with the four
exits.

The *pastorie* lies adjacent both to the church, to which it is physically
joined, and to the forecourt. It overlaps the south east corner of the
trapeze which forms the main building and lies parallel to the reception
complex on the other side of the building. Doors give access to the private
garden, to the rear access road (via the garage and parking lot),and to the
forecourt. The main doorway, set square into the building to provide a
porch, is of slightly smaller dimensions than the entrances to the church
and has only one door (as opposed to three doors for the front entrances
to the church and two doors for each of the rear entrances). Its smaller
scale and the single door characterize it as /private/ rather than /public/.
The internal division of space, like that of the reception complex and the
sacristies, is rectangular, except where the angulation of the building
necessitates pentagonal rooms. An unmarked wooden door gives interior
access to the church from the *pastorie*. It appears to be kept locked.
In figure 14 we give a summary of the positions and oppositions.

1.2. Orientation

With orientation, we are looking at two things: first, how the different
spaces may be oriented to one another and second how individual spaces
may be oriented by the presence of one or more poles. In a church, interior

Summary *Positions and Oppositions*

1. Vertical Plane:
    ++ ceiling height of main church (9-10)
    +2 minister's chairs
    +1 sanctuaries (10) and (6)
     0 (9), (4), (5), (7)
    -1 – – –
    -2 baptistry (8)

2. Horizontal plane:

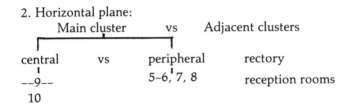

FIGURE 14

Orientation is complex because of the number of different *topoi* within the building. On the basis of our analysis of position, and anticipating our analysis of narrative programs, we can identify three major spaces: the church, the *pastorie*, and the reception complex.

1.2.1. In the reception complex, rooms 22-26 are oriented to (19) and, less obviously, to the church. The main reception room (19) is not itself oriented by any other room and has no fixed pole to provide interior orientation: it is a multipurpose space.

1.2.2. The *pastorie* is even more complex, but it can be left aside since it is not part of the public space.

1.2.3. The church itself has a number of areas with their own spatial programming, all linked by the transition area (4).

1.2.3.1 In the main church there is both vertical and horizontal orientation.

Vertical orientation is provided by the pillars on the ground level, by the roof supports curving up from the corbels to meet at the central roof beam, by the plain, coloured wall hangings on the rear wall each side of (11), by the organ pipes, and by the crucifix mounted on top of the free-standing wall behind (10). Countering the upward thrust of the pillars, however, is the strong horizontal line of the white lintels, and once the roof-supports reach the roof they disappear visually into the ceiling which is of the same coloured wood. The coloured wall hangings, though long and narrow, hang below the line of the lintels and, with their square tops, do not succeed in pointing beyond it. Only the crucifix and the organ pipes offer a strong vertical thrust. Even so, the figure on the crucifix curves back down towards the earth and the upward thrust of the organ pipes is partly contained by the casing which boxes them in.

A mild contrast between /above/ and /below/ is offered by the raised platform of (10), but since this is only one step up and since it increases visibility for those seated in (9), it marks the opposition between (9) and (10) without accentuating it. The same may be said of the ministers' chairs which are raised a further step, enabling their occupants to see and to be seen across the altar. Thus they serve to accentuate the horizontal lines of the space, rather than challenging them.

Most characteristic of this building is the use of embedding. The exterior walls of the church, including the low walls along the front of the forecourt, constitute a broken hexagon. Not only is this motif reflected in the pattern of paving in the forecourt, but it is repeated inside the building in the shape of the main congregational area (9) and, embedded within that, in the shape of the sanctuary. The sanctuary, in turn, contains moveable chairs for the ministers and a moveable lectern for the reader, but is actually focussed on the fixed stone altar which occupies the most prominent position in (10). Thus the altar stands immoveably at the center of a series of concentric hexagons and serves as a pole for the whole building.

In (9) the seating arrangement is unmistakably oriented towards (10), but without excluding a view of the rest of the congregation who surround (10) on five of its six sides. The only exception is the organist's seat, facing away from (9) and (10), but this anti-orientation is neutralized by the provision of a mirror.

1.2.3.2. The *dagkapel* also consists of two spaces, one oriented the other orienting, but here they are juxtaposed over against each other instead of being embedded. The seating and kneelers of the congregational space faces one way: towards the altar and tabernacle in (6). Face-to-face sighting of other members of the congregation is excluded. The altar, from its placement in the sanctuary space and from the arrangement of candles, bookstand, etc. on its top, clearly faces the people. Behind it, and visible over it, is the glass tabernacle, whose shape – an elongated hexagon with shallow pitched roof – reflects that of the upper level of the church itself. Thus, there are two foci competing for visual attention from (5): the altar and the tabernacle. When the altar is not in use and especially when the, spotlight is turned on, the tabernacle is the dominant visual focus.

1.2.3.3. The baptistry is centered on the font. Wooden benches affixed to the wall orientate participants to the font. The presence of the paschal candle further privileges the font.

1.2.3.4. The *devotieruimte* has a double orientation: to the Russian icon on the left and to the baroque madonna and child on the right. Votive lights stand between both, while a one-meter tall candlestick to the right of the madonna holds a large white candle. No fixed seating or kneelers are provided.

It is the orientation provided by the icon, statue, candle and votive lights which defines this area, since there are no boundaries between it and the transition area (4).

1.2.3.5. The transition space (4) links a series of subspaces which, even more than the *devotieruimte*, rely on their polarity rather than any physical or visual boundary for their definition.

4a. Memorials of deceased parishioners. Inside the long south-east wall of the church and along the wall that separates the church from the reception complex are niches, covering the walls from top to bottom and each containing identical wooden crosses on which the names of deceased parishioners are painted. Here and there, votive candles, small bouquets of flowers, even children's drawings, indicate that these crosses win the attention of those attending this church.

(In contrast to these names of the dead on the outer wall, the pillars of the inner space (9) are adorned with reproductions of the icons of unidentified saints, with an icon of Christ at the center, facing the ministers. These icons are placed just above eye level and face inward to the sanctuary, over the heads of the congregation. Since the seating abuts right up to the pillars, it is not in fact possible to stand before these icons, whose purpose seems more to help define the congregational space than to become the focus of devotion.)

4b. Stations of the Cross. On the same external wall between the baptistry and the *devotieruimte*, fourteen bronze plaques are set side by side at eye height. They are grouped in three clusters, – near the baptistry, in the middle of the wall, and near the *devotieruimte* – separated by the memorials of the dead. Each plaque is inscribed with one or two words, sufficient to identify the plaques as being the Stations of the Cross.

4c. Bookshelves. In the transition area (4), a bookshelf with hymnals is mounted on the pillar nearest each of the four entrances. The only exception is entrance B, where the shelves are mounted on the wall behind (7).

4d. Literature. Next to the most northerly angled pillar between (9) and (4), on the side facing entrance (A), a small table offers parish newsletters and other literature, including reading material for younger children. Similarly near entrance B, where a small table on the left of the entrance offers printed leaflets and a few books for sale.

4e. Holy water. Just inside entrance (A), on the left, and just inside entrance (B) on the right, small bronze holy water stoups are hung on a nail in the wall. Similar stoups are also to be found near entrances (C) and (D).

4f. Hat-stand. Next to the holy water stoup at entrance B there is a hat-stand and an umbrella-stand, presumably for those who, using this entrance, do not avail themselves of the more defined cloakroom-space (23), near entrance A.

4g. St. Joseph statue. Near the angle of the wall where the *dagkapel* meets the *pastorie* a somewhat smaller than lifesize statue of St. Joseph stands on a plinth. There is little sign that it provides any significant orientation.

1.3. Summary

1.3.1. There is little vertical orientation in this church. The only two areas so marked are the main church, where there is some heavily compromised /upward/ thrust, and the baptistry which has a modest /downward/ thrust provided by the two steps down into it.

Significant horizontal orientation was found throughout the church, in contrast to the reception room itself which orients the adjacent rooms but is not itself oriented. Within the church, we can distinguish three classes of orientation:

centripetal	bi-directional	uni-directional
or		
(9) → (10)	(5) → (6)	all poles in (4)
(8) → font		

FIGURE 15

Moreover, the directions of the different orientations are such that certain narrative programs are spatially and temporally incompatible. Thus those seated in (5) are ill-placed to participate in a liturgy celebrated in (9) and (10), and vice versa. Private devotion to the Blessed Sacrament is clearly separated from private devotion to Mary or Joseph, as these are separated from each other. Similarly, the celebration of baptism in the baptistry renders it physically and visually inaccessible to a congregation gathered in (9).

1.3.2. If we combine the findings with regard to position and those relating to orientation, we find the following:

	Orientation				Position				
	vertical		horizontal		height	embedding		linkage	boundaries
	up	down	space	pole		cntr	peri		
9)	+		+	+	+	+	+		+
10)				+	+	+			+
5)			+	+		+			+
6)				+		+			+
4)						+			
7)				+		+			
8)		+		+		+			+
4a)				+		+			
4b)				+		+			
4c)				+		+			
4d)				+		+			
4e)				+		+			
4f)				+		+			
4g)				+		+			

FIGURE 16

2. PLASTIC CATEGORIES

2.1. Chromatics

Light and colour in built spaces serve both to facilitate the subjects in the performance of their various programs and to accentuate topoi associated with the main actantial roles.

2.1.1. *Light*

Natural light
The only unfiltered direct light comes through the ring of windows in the
upper level of the main church (9). This clerestory is the strongest source
of natural light and certainly privileges the area (main church) that it illuminates. It is also the only source of natural light that comes from
above. (In fact, the altar is located on the north-west side of (9) and faces
south-east, so that when the morning sun shines through the windows of
the upper level it falls on the sanctuary area.) Unfiltered light also comes
indirectly through the doorways, since the doors are of glass, but this
only illuminates areas of (4) close to each exit.

Filtered natural light is also provided in two forms: through the stained
glass of the windows in the baptistery and adjacent to the *devotieruimte*,
and through the curtained windows in the *dagkapel*, the reception area,
and the sacristies. Thus we can recognize a certain hierarchical system of
natural lighting:

full	9, 10	=	high intensity
filtered	5, 6		
coloured	7, 8		
indirect	4	=	low intensity

FIGURE 17

Artificial lighting
Artificial *lighting* is provided in the form of candles and of the electrical
lighting system. Candles are associated with various poles: the altars
(6,10), the icon and statue of the BVM (7), the font (8) and the memorials of
dead. Electrical lights serve either practical or spotlighting functions. The
tabernacle in (6) is spotlighted, the baptismal font is illuminated by a cluster
of three hexagonal lamps, the altar area is illuminated by nine lamps set
into the ceiling above it, and by a spotlight mounted on a roofbeam. In
contrast, the congregational area is lit by a row of lamps set into the high
ceiling, one in front of each window. Similar functional lighting is provided
in the weekday chapel, in the transition area and in the entrance ways.

2.1.2. *Colour*

Unsaturated colours
Natural colours dominate: sand-coloured bricks of walls and columns;
natural woods in the roof, roof-supports, organ casing and doorframes;
grey granite in the consecration crosses, grey-brown stone slabs in the

sanctuary floor, and blocks of light grey granite in the altar, with a dark grey marble *mensa*. The wooden lectern is painted to match the grey of the altar. In (4) and (8), hexagonal pebbled tiles provide the flooring. Off-white concrete lintels run around the inside of (9), marking the lower level off from the upper level. Similarly muted man-made materials are used in the flooring of the congregational space: off-white vinyl flooring, with black vinyl flooring used to demarcate the boundary between (9) and (4). The choice of flooring represents a discreet but systematic way of differentiating the congregational space (vinyl) from the sanctuary area (stone) and from the other spaces (pebble tiles).

Saturated colours
Saturated colours are found in permanent items in the church: the brass and glass door of the reliquary set into the front of the altar and incorporating the parish logo (cross, sword and key); the white altar cloths; the icons mounted on the pillars of (9) and the icon of Mary in the *devotieruimte*; the stained glass in (7) and (8); the green hymnbooks. There are also changeable items that introduce saturated colours into the space: plants and flowers by the altar and lectern and on the wall behind the ministers' seats; flowers by the statue of the BVM; wall hangings either side of (11) which vary according to feast and season. Small sprigs of flowers are also to be found from time to time in the various niches of the memorials of the parish dead.

2.1.3. *Summary*

There is very little saturated colour in the building. The sand-coloured brickwork forms all the vertical planes (walls), while a range of shades from black to dark grey to off white and textures (pebbled vs smooth) differentiates floor space. Floor-space is differentiated as follows:

(9) off-white vinyl flooring vs (10) dark grey-brown stone, boundary marked by a step;
(9) off-white vinyl flooring vs (4) off-white pebble tiles boundary marked by band of black vinyl.
Other areas are not differentiated by floor-colour.

FIGURE 18

Saturated colours mark the baptistry and devotional area (stained glass windows), the main church (wall hangings and icons) and particular poles (flowers). Spotlights and candles mark most of the same locations.

The pattern of use of light and colour can be displayed as follows:

	Light		Colour [2]			
	Natural		Artificial		marking	
	full	filter [3]	candles	spots	pole	space
9	+					+
10	+		+	+	+	+
5		+				
6			+	+	+	
4						
7			+	+	+	
8			+	+		
4						
4a			*		*	
4b						
4c					+	
4d						
4e						
4f					+	
4g			+			

FIGURE 19

* Since these light and flowers are provided by private individuals and not by the church it seems best to treat them as belonging to a different, non-spatial system.

2.2. Eidetics

Four fundamental shapes give rise to the various configurations:

hexagon: perfect –   (8), and font in (8)
               elongated –   (9), (10) and tabernacle in (6)
               broken –   configuration of whole building plus courtyard
trapeze   (half-hexagon):   ministers' platform, superimposed upon

3. Unsaturated colours are omitted from this chart since they form the general chromatic background for the use of saturated colours. Consequently, the remarks on floor-colour made above are registered here under 'marking boundaries'.
4. In the text we included 'colour' (vs 'uncoloured') and 'indirect' vs 'direct' as oppositions. The second opposition remains, but we retain only the marked term 'direct', since all other light in the building is indirect. The first opposition is dropped, since the stained glass windows belong more to the category of colour than of light.

the whole hexagon that is (10); church including *dagkapel*, which is half of the hexagon constituted by the outer walls of the church plus the rectory and the walls of the courtyard

pentagon: sanctuary of the weekday chapel (6), storage space (21), rooms (30) and (31) in *pastorie*

rectangle: reception room (19), storage space (20), cloakroom and toilets (22-26), rooms in *pastorie* (30-38), sacristies; windows and doors.

FIGURE 20

These shapes are themselves configurations and could be broken down into elementary units based on the degree of the angle, i.e 45, 60, or 72-degree angles. It is not easy to see what would be gained thereby.

2.3. Summary

While no obvious system, no 'phonetics' of the building has yet appeared, we can summarize our progress so far by categorizing the oppositions we have found to be present in the elements of the form of the expression:

position:	vertical	/above/vs/below/
	horizontal	/inclusion/vs/juxtaposition/
		/embedding/vs/embedded/
orientation:	vertical	/upwards/vs/downwards/
	horizontal	/centripetal/vs/linear/
		/unidirectional/vs/bidirectional
		/oriented to a space/vs/oriented to a pole/
light	natural	/direct/vs/indirect/
		/full/ vs/filtered/
	artificial	/focussed/vs/diffused/
		/candlelight/vs/spotlight/
colour	saturated	/spatial/vs/polarizing/
	unsaturated	/spatial/vs/polarizing/

eidetics   hexagon vs trapeze   (/whole/vs/part/)
                        vs
                 pentagon
                        vs
                 rectangle

FIGURE 21

B. THE FORM OF THE CONTENT

With the form of the content we shift from the building as a complex of signifiers to the messages or 'meaning-effects' given off by the building. Retracing the generative trajectory, we begin with the discursive level, the level at which the enunciator (the person or persons responsible for the design) organizes the meaning. The discursive level has both semantic units (figures and themes) and syntactic networks (their organization). It is here that traces of the enunciation, the original production of the building as a 'statement' intended for a specific audience, might appear.

1. THE LEVEL OF DISCOURSIVE STRUCTURES

1.1. Discoursive Syntax

A text is always an 'utterance' whose surface construction arranges the contents in various frameworks or 'scenes' marked by a certain unity of time, place and actors. The same is true of an architectural 'utterance' whose production is largely organized in terms of the various kinds of activity that will take place there and the occasions on which it is intended to be used, and people thought likely to use it and the respective roles they are likely to play in using the building. In each of these dimensions – actorial, temporal and spatial – it is possible, though not always likely, that some traces of the original enunciation may be discovered.

1.1.1. *Actorialization and Temporalization*

The building bears no trace of the enunciator. Built into the pillar nearest the main entrance (A) there is a foundation stone with the inscription: "Petrus-Steenrots draag dit werk. Schraag het volk Gods. Sterk Uw kerk. 6-29-1969 +" ("Peter-Rock support this work. Support God's people. Strengthen Your Church. 6-29-1969 +"). Among the memorial crosses on the south-east wall is one for Johannes Lelieveldt, with the nota "architect dezer kerk" ("architect of this church").[5] Curiously, there is no inscription of the name or title of the church either inside or outside the building. The

---

5. See 3.1.1., note 5.

name commonly given to area (5) and (6) – '*dagkapel*' – is also found on the blueprints and might therefore be said to be an instance of temporal programming: a chapel for weekday use.

1.1.2. *Spatialization*

The spatial meanings of the building can be analysed in two ways: first, insofar as the building consists of a 'here' over against a 'there' and, within the 'here', differentiates between primary and secondary spaces; second, insofar as the design and interior arrangement of the building constitute a program for certain kinds of activities while excluding others.

1.1.3.1. *Spatial localization*
The distinction between topic and heterotopic spaces ('here' vs 'there') is entirely relative. Nonetheless, in opposition to the church site, the surrounding residential area is heterotopic. In relation to the interior of the church, the exterior forecourt and surrounding lawns, parking, etc., are heterotopic. In the context of Sunday Eucharist, the areas (9) and (10) are topic while the weekday chapel, the reception complex, and the *pastorie* are heterotopic, as are the baptistry and the *devotieruimte*.

But more can be said. The building is designed to accommodate a limited number of activities. These activities can be grouped in terms of main activities and subordinate activities and find a corresponding grouping of main spaces (utopic), with their respective poles, and support areas (paratopic spaces) (figure 22, see page 111)

The *pastorie*, like any domestic residence, is designed for a number of performances and thus has a series of utopic spaces (dining room, bedrooms, sitting rooms, parlours) and corresponding paratopic spaces (kitchen, bathrooms, toilets, closets, entranceway, passageways). Note that (49) – the boiler room – is paratopic to the whole building and all its programs.

1.1.3.2. *Spatial Programming*
Spatial programming refers to the way the utopic and paratopic spaces are connected with one another to form a series of spatial sequences which thus determine the behavioral patterns of those who use the building.

If we begin with the four entrances (or five if the private door to the *pastorie* is included), it is immediately apparent that two basic sequences emerge (figure 23):

utopic spaces	poles	paratopic spaces
A. (10)	altar lectern pres. chair	(23) cloakroom & toilets (30) - (29) **pastorie** (12) - (14) sacristies (15) - (16) toilet
(9)	seats organ	(19) choir rehearsal (13) storeroom (A) - (D) entranceways (4) walkway/transition
B. (8) baptistry	font	as above
C. (7) **devotieruimte**	icon statue	(4) and (A) to (D)
D. (5) - (6) **dagkapel**	altar	NP 'weekdays Mass': as above
	tabernacle	NP 'visits to BlSacr': (4) and (A) - (D)
E. (19) reception		(A) and (D) (20) - (21) storerooms (22) buffet (23) cloakroom (25) - (26)

FIGURE 22

A > (1) > (4)   or   A > (1) > 23
B > (2) > (4)
C > (3) > (4)
D > (17) > (4)   or   D > (17) > 19
pastorie > (4)

FIGURE 23

Thus, while the two southern entrances and that from the *pastorie* only give access to the church, the northern entrances offer a choice: either the church or the reception area.

The reception area thus forms a sequence of spaces independent of the church, with (23) being pivotal but not the exclusive point of entry into the main reception room (19).

Within the church, it is the transition area (4) which is pivotal: no area can be reached without passing through (4). Nonetheless, (4) gives access not only to individual sub-spaces, such as (7) and (8), but also to the following clusters:

utopic spaces: weekday chapel: (4) – (5)
utopic spaces: main church: (9) – (10)
paratopic spaces: sacristies : (12) – (16)

It is to be noted that the sacristies are independently linked to the main church through (11), whereas they are linked to other utopic spaces, such as (6), (7), and (8), only via (4). This suggests a closer link between the main church and the sacristies than between the sacristies and the other performances they support.

Interestingly, no sequence is established between the various utopic spaces themselves: the baptistry, the *devotieruimte*, the weekday chapel, the main church and the various *topoi* arranged along the northern and south-eastern walls of (4) are not in any way connected with each other. The only one of these poles to include its own spatial programming is the Stations of the Cross, whose numbering programs movement from one plaque to the next, beginning near the baptistry and ending near the *devotieruimte*, though without any significant connection with either of these two utopic spaces.

The paratopic subspaces in (4), – the hatstand, the hymnbook shelves, the holy water stoups – are located in spots designed to make their services readily accessible to those entering and leaving the church. The cloakrooms (23-26), on the other hand, require a deliberate detour for visitors to the church, as does the reception complex as a whole. However, these last remarks already move us on to the next section.

1.1.3.3. *Spatial aspectualization*
Spatial aspectualization is said to be the transformation of the activity of a subject of the utterance into qualitative spatial movement, either physical or visual. In analysing a given space (either a natural or a constructed space), the presence of a fictitious 'actant observateur' is postulated, – a hypothetical observer from whose perspective the relationship between spaces, or objects in space, is evaluated in terms of distance to be crossed and possible barriers to such passage, or in terms of visibility, as these impose themselves on subjects occupying such spaces.

a. *Visual aspectualization*
For the visitor entering though the main entrance, the main church (9-10) is immediately visible, and everything else is for the moment hidden. Entering through door B, the visitor sees both the main church and the weekday chapel. Coming in through the rear entrances, C and D, the visitor at first sees only part of (4), but the light coming from the upper storey windows quickly draws the eye to the main church.

If we locate our hypothetical observer in the congregational area of the main church, the following aspectualizations hold good:

1. The *pastorie* and the reception area are totally out of sight.
2. The sacristies are also out of sight, but the concealed entrance (11) is visible.
3. To anyone facing (10), all other areas are visually inaccessible (behind one's back) or visually remote.
4. The various poles in (10) – the altar, the lectern and the ministers (though not their chairs) are easily visible, even when the congregational area is full of people. Those in the back row are no further from the sanctuary than people in the back row of (5) are from (6).
5. From any point in (9), the presence of other members of the congregation is easily visible.
6. The choir is not a visually distinct section of the congregation when it is not performing.

With regard to the other spaces, we should only add that the congregation in the *dagkapel* is so organized that members are unable to see each other's faces, but all can see the altar and tabernacle. The other devotional areas in (4), including (7) similarly focus attention away from other people and towards the pole. Conversely, in the baptistry, all who face the pole (font) will also see other participants across the space.

	Barriers to physical access				
	solid walls	doors		steps	none
		closed	open		
(9)					+
(10)				+	
(5)					+
(6)				+	+
(7)				+	+
(8)					+
choir					
(12 - 14)	+	+			
(17)	+		+		
pastorie	+		+		
hallways			+		

FIGURE 24

b. *Physical aspectualization*
Physical access from one space to another is either open or restricted. In this church, restrictions on physical access are placed by solid wall, wooden or glass doors, and steps. The easiest way to describe the patterns of access is to display them in the form of a chart (figure 24, see page 113).

It is also worth remarking upon the fact that there are four entrances to the church and no central entrance, just as there are five aisles giving access to the congregational seating and three entrances to the sacristies. All the sacristy entrances are hidden from the view of those in (9) and none is visually more important than another. The same lack of differentiation attends the aisles in (9): there is no distinction between 'main aisle' and 'side aisles'.

In terms of *hearing*, it is interesting that microphones are provided in (10) but not in (9), while speakers are located in (9) but not in (10). This suggests an opposition between (10) as the place of the enunciator and (9) as the place of the enunciatee, or at least between an individual enunciator in (10) and a collective enunciatee (and sometimes enunciator) in (9). The size of the other spaces renders amplifying systems unnecessary, even if they are the *topoi* of programs that include speaking aloud.

1.1.4. *Summary of Discoursive Syntax*

In analysing the discoursive syntax, we have been analysing the way the enunciator, in enunciating the building, has organized its overall space as a topical space, segmenting the whole into parts that are related to each other physically and visually in series of combinations and oppositions: utopic and paratopic spaces, various configurations of spaces and their relationship to each other, the kinds of physical and visual dividers and connectors that join or separate spaces from each other. But these spaces are not merely abstract, geometrical configurations: the spaces are also places in which people move and which they occupy. Such occupancy and use is possible because the spaces are recognizeable places, habitats of different kinds which have a position in the lexicon of human habitation but which are realized in a new and unique way in any given building. From the lexicon of discoursive spatial memory, visitors are able to identify the kind of place they are entering. In so doing, they are identifying the figures of spatial discourse, and in recognizing the building as a coherent and distinctive whole, they are picking up on its themes. We have now to analyse how this is possible in the case of the church of SS. Peter and Paul.

1.2. Discoursive Semantics

1.2.1. *Figures and Figurative Trajectories*

If we ask what the building looks like from the inside, the answer is perfectly obvious: it looks like a church. More specifically, the figures are all those associated with 'Catholic church'. But what are the clues that give rise to this recognition? The clues are the various figures, which are grasped not in isolation but in their connectedness with one another in various groupings or trajectories.

1. The church is a 'place of assembly': its entranceways are larger than those of private dwellings, it has seating for 400 people, and that seating is arranged, not for simultaneous private performances, as in a restaurant or cinema, but for public interaction among those who attend. The public character of the place is also indicated by the high ceiling of the central area, as opposed to the low ceilings of the peripheral areas.

2. It is a 'place of formal proceedings', as witnessed by the raised platform at the center of the assembly, with its chairs facing the assembly, its lectern, and its fixed, uncluttered altar-table. The microphones and loudspeakers in the ceiling also indicate that the assembly is intended to be an orderly one, as do the hymnboards which suggest that the proceedings are planned and not spontaneous.

3. It is also a 'place for private prayer and devotion', as witnessed by its *devotieruimte*, its Stations of the Cross, its statue of St. Joseph.

4. It is a 'place for speaking and singing'. It has a lectern, microphones, and an organ. Hymnbooks are provided and hymnboards indicate what is to be sung.

5. It is a 'place for sacramental actions'. The discoursive memory of Catholics, at least, will recognize the two altars, the tabernacle, the font, the aumbry. (But they will look in vain for a confessional!)

6. It is a 'place connected with a tradition', as the presence of Eastern icons and the baroque madonna show. The connectedness with tradition is also expressed by the presence of the crucifix, the altar and font, the tabernacle, and so forth, though these are all 'modern' in style. More recent tradition is expressed by the memorials for dead parishioners which occupy the two longest walls of the church.

7. Many of the items mentioned contribute to the 'religious' identity of the place, especially the holy water stoups at the entrances, the icons on the pillars of the main area, and the altar and crucifix at the center. Some

of the literature, such as the biblical storybooks for children, also plays into this trajectory, as do the stained glass windows.

8.   The specific 'Catholic' character of the place is not strongly evident, but is suggested by the reservation of the eucharist and the kneelers provided in (5), by the shrine to Mary, the practice of prayer for the dead, the literature relating to diocesan programs, the photographs of overseas missionaries.

9.   'Community life' is another trajectory. It is constituted by the presence of the reception area and adjacent facilities which make informal gatherings possible, as well as by the seating of the congregation in the round, the announcements of forthcoming events in the parish, the city and the diocese, the signs of money-raising efforts to support the church and parish, and occasional notices regarding the pastoral council or the children of the parish.

10.   'Quality of life': the aesthetic quality of the building and its furnishings, the obvious care with which plants and flowers are arranged and positioned, the quality of the organ; all these combine with posters announcing musical events and posters and literature relating to 'het conciliair proces'[6] to create a trajectory of 'concern for quality of life'.

Some of these figures belong to isotopies that are incidental to the building as an architectural whole (e.g. those realized in literary form in posters and notices), while others are spatially quite peripheral. If we ask what figurative isotopy dominates the architectural ensemble and does the most to relate the figurative trajectories to each other, we shall have to answer 'public worship'. That is the dominant *figurative isotopy*. Perhaps, alongside it, we should also place the isotopy of 'contemporary tradition', since so many of the figures combine 'traditional' with 'contemporary'.

1.2.2. *Themes and Thematic Trajectories*

However familiar and recognizeable these trajectories might be, their arrangement is such as to produce a new contextualization for them: this is not a 'classical' or 'traditional' church. This contextualization is the key to the uniqueness and originality of the building and can be identified by examination of the themes or categories of opposing values which give the figures their semantic organization.

---

6. The 'conciliar process' concerns a program of the christian churches for social justice, peace and integrity of the creation.

1.   A first and most striking opposition is that between 'communal celebrations' associated with the main space and 'quasi-communal celebrations' associated with the peripheral spaces (5-6) and (8), which provide for performances which are more than individual but less than truly communal. This opposition belongs to a category we might call 'public events' in contrast to spaces intended exclusively for 'private devotions'. The organization of the respective spaces in the latter category ('public' vs 'private') is also marked by the opposition between 'fixed order' and 'private initiative' (e.g. in the presence or absence of fixed seating and other indicators of prescribed patterns of intersubjective interaction).

2.   Two of the three spaces clearly designated for communal or quasi-communal events, the main church and the *dagkapel*, are further differentiated by the contrast between a space for the performance of the many and the space for the performance of the few: we can label this opposition 'community act' vs 'ministerial act'. The fact that the opposition is marked by a raised platform, thus an opposition between /above/ and /below/, indicates that the opposition 'community' vs 'ministers' is a hypotactic one of 'determined' vs 'determining', thus a hierarchical one of 'superior' vs 'inferior'. Interestingly enough, the third space in this group of 'public' spaces, the baptistry, does not figurativize any such opposition.

3.   The contrast between (4) as a transitional space leading to the fixed seating arrangements in (9) and (5) also sets up an opposition between 'crowd' and 'community', as between a virtual and an actualized collective actant.

4.   The presence of referential figures from the past (the crucified Christ, Mary, the saints, the names of deceased parishioners) and of traditional objects like altars and holy water stoups is in contrast to the living people who use the church and to the modern style in which these traditional objects are presented. There is also the contrast between 'biblical' literature and writings and posters concerning the present or the immediate future. This gives rise to a pervasive thematic trajectory of 'time', with the oppositions 'tradition' vs 'modernity'.

5.   Similarly, there is also a spatial theme within the interior which situates the occupants in relation to poles that are either in front of them or in the midst of them. As we saw in looking at the various kinds of orientation, the devotional areas and the weekday chapel set up a confrontation between the pole and the persons who conjoin themselves to the area of the pole, whereas in the baptistry and in the main church, the pole is either central or off-center but in both cases embedded in its respective *topos*. This sets up an opposition between spaces which put the object of value (and/or the enunciatee) 'in the midst' of the assembled subjects and those

which put it 'beyond' the assembled subjects or the individual subject.

6. Finally, the contrast between the living and the dead, the opposition between subjects who are present in the flesh and subjects who are 'represented' by means of some referentializing or iconic figure (written names, statues, eucharistic bread) set up another thematic opposition between 'this worldly' and 'other worldly'. Throughout the devotional areas and the *dagkapel*, this opposition is played out on a horizontal axis: the believer faces the statue of Mary, or the tabernacle, or the memorial of the dead. Similarly in the main area, where altar and lectern face the people. However, one wonders whether the same opposition might not also be figured in the /above/ vs /below/ of the main church: the above being an empty unstructured space which is source of light, in opposition to the full, structured space on which it sheds its light.

These oppositions summarize the characteristic ways in which this church handles the received tradition of providing a building for public worship. Its characteristic features can be seen all the more clearly in comparison with 'classical' churches. The roundness of the central congregational space and the way it encloses and includes the sanctuary area, makes this clearly a space that is intended for events in which all those in attendance are involved in what is going on. The liturgy is led by a leader, instead of being conducted in semi-privacy on behalf of the people and out of range of their sight and hearing. A clear distinction is also made between this public space and other functions that may occur in the church, such as private devotions (Stations of the Cross, prayer to Mary) or small-group activities (baptism, weekday Mass). These are removed, literally, to the periphery and are out of sight of those gathered in the main space. While it does not lack elements of the 'transcendent' or 'sacred' (particularly the icons and statues), these are kept rather discreet, contained within the human space rather than breaking out of it. Similarly, while it maintains the practice of marking role differentiation in spatial terms, it clearly strives to incorporate such differentiations within the unity of the whole assembly, and to minimize the hierarchical implications of such distinctions.

The arrangement of the seating not only is such as to surround and enclose the sanctuary; it also means that congregants see each others' faces instead of only the backs of the heads of the people in front of them. Similarly, in contrast to the linear orientation of the traditional church, whose lines lead the eye beyond the congregation and even beyond the priest to some transcendent 'beyond', the arrangement of a church 'in the round' brings the focus of attention back into the midst of the assembly, back to the empty space at its center which is filled only in the course of the rite itself, by the ministers and the *sacra* (Word and gifts) which focus and complete the assembly.

The thematic isotopies seem to privilege the human NP over the divine NP, human presence over divine presence, the 'here' rather than the 'there'. It was the much earlier move to accentuate the transcendent over the community, the divine action in the liturgy over the human ritual event, the 'real' presence of Christ over the 'attendance' of the people, which led to the celebrant facing away from the people, to moving the bishop's throne to one side, to proclaiming the Gospel to the north. Now the positions have been reversed again. The 'sacred/profane' dichotomy is abandoned and the human quality of the ritual events is highlighted by the scale of the space, the relative continuity between sanctuary and congregational space, the provision that all in the congregation will be able to see and hear and respond with ease. The provision of paratopic spaces for the members of the congregation – cloakrooms, toilets, and a reception area, unknown in traditional churches – are another indication of this building's *humanitas*.

Yet, for all that, the tension between the 'transcendent' and the 'immanent' is not dissolved, merely restated or re-discoursivized. For this reason, the dominant *thematic isotopy* seems to be the tension between what is 'in the midst of the assembly' and what is 'beyond' it.

2. THE SURFACE LEVEL

The semio-narrative structures are the basic relations and transformations of relations which underlie the more elaborated figures and themes (and their organization) at the discursive level. In looking at a building, we are looking at the relationships which the building sets up between different kinds of occupants and users of that building. In particular, we are looking at the various *topoi* (sing. *topos*: a given space which, in relation to another space, invests the occupants with certain competences in relation to the occupants of the other space.)

2.1. Narrative Syntax

The various sections into which the building's interior arrangements divide its total space are endowed with different syntactic roles. At the discursive level, we have already designated them 'utopic' and 'paratopic' (cfr 1.1.3.1 Spatial localization, supra). Now we move to the semio-narrative structures which underlie the discursive organization of space, looking particularly at how these spaces define the actantial roles and at the modal or descriptive values which are joined to those actantial roles in virtue of the space in which those roles are assumed. It should be emphasized here that the relationship between space and actantial roles and values is not one-to-one, but rather a correlation of a configuration of roles on the one hand and a spatial configuration on the other.

We can simplify matters by excluding from consideration the whole *pastorie* and the reception area (19-26), since these are visually and physically inaccessible to those who come to the church to take part in the narrative programs for which it was intended.

2.1.1. *Several topoi*

Within the main area of the interior, we can differentiate several *topoi* belonging to distinct narrative programs. Thus the area of the *dagkapel* is differentiated from the main area of 9-10 by its separate seating arrangement, different orientation, independent lighting, and the two sets of pillars which mark the boundaries of 9 and 5 respectively and between which is the transition area 4. The *devotieruimte*, the memorials of the dead, the stations of the cross are all continuous with (4), but narrative programs requiring conjunction with these objects involve turning one's back to the main area (9). Similarly, the baptistry is a distinct area, separated from (9) by (4) and marked off from (4) by being sunk to a level two steps below the rest of the floor area, by the low wall and by its independent lighting. The congregation in (9) has its back to the baptistry.

Because of the clear separation of the different utopic areas, each of them needs to be analyzed separately, but we shall focus here on the area of the main church: (9) and (10).

2.1.2. *The sanctuary area and the congregational area*

We have already seen that the sanctuary area (10) is embedded in the congregational area (9), being surrounded by the congregation (including the choir) on three sides, and detached from the back wall of the church so as to be thrust into the congregational space. This yields two distinct topical spaces indicating two distinct sets of roles and competencies within a joint narrative program.

Of itself, this arrangement is capable of being used for a number of quite different narrative programs: for theater in the round, for judicial proceedings, for parliamentary debates, for academic lectures. In each instance, the division of the space between the embedded *topos* and the embedding *topos* would set up a corresponding allocation of modal competencies in view of the particular performances to be undertaken there. The specific narrative program for which it is in fact designed, however, is indicated by the simultaneous presence of the chairs for the presider and assistants, the lectern, and the altar in (10). These represent three poles which are poles for both (9) and (10): they govern both spaces in virtue of either physical conjunction or audio-visual conjunction. Conversely, the chairs and the organ in (9) represent two poles which govern both (9) and (10) in virtue of either physical, visual or auditory conjunction.

These three poles of (10) create three corresponding *topoi*, all of which are contained within (10). The only clear line of demarcation between the *topoi* is the single step up to the chairs from the level on which altar and lectern stand. This suggests that the competence and performance associated with the presider's chair is on a hierarchically different level from the performances associated with lectern and altar, perhaps something of a hyponymic relationship of a category to its two terms. Moreover, the fact that the altar is central and the lectern stands to one side suggests that, while the NPs carried out at the altar and lectern are on the same plane, that of the lectern is oriented to that of the altar and not vice versa.

Having said that, the relationship between the two spaces, (9) and (10) cannot be understood without reference to the actors who assume these different spaces. In M. Hammad's words: "The topical arrangement governs the structure of actantial roles in terms of power (pouvoir)". His research suggests, he says, a correspondence not between actant and topos or NP and topos, but between 'topical arrangement' and 'modal structures of power'. In other words, the spatial differentiation of the actors also denotes a social differentiation. Spatial distribution is correlated with the distribution of competence in a program which is one of intersubjective interaction involving distinct (if shifting) actantial roles. Perhaps the best way to proceed to an analysis of such topical arrangements and their respective 'modal structures of power' is to take each of the poles in turn.

2.1.3. Presider's chair

There is a mutual orientation of the presider's chair and the seating of the congregation, but it is a hypotactic relationship in that the presider's chair defines the assembly and not vice versa: only when it is occupied is the assembly in session. The narrative programs associated with the chair in the course of the liturgy have largely to do with the instituting and dissolution of the assembly as a collective actant:

opening rites:	formation of the collective actant – (10) manipulates and (9) acquiesces;
creed and prayers of the faithful:	maintenance of collective actant: (10) initiates joint performances with (9) which affirm the 'fiduciary contract' underlying the formation of the collective actant;
concluding rites:	dissolution of assembly initiated by (10) and acquiesced in by (9).

Thus, the configuration of (9)-(10) as polarized by the presidential chair over against the congregational seating corresponds to a competence to institute the collective actant over against the competence to be instituted as a collective actant. The first competence is acquired by conjunction with the presider's chair, the second by conjunction with the undifferentiated congregational seating, but neither competence exists independently of the other: even if the priest sits on his chair, there is no assembly unless the members of the congregation take their place. Similarly, even though the faithful are in their seats, the assembly is not in session until the priest takes his. Moreover, the priest is not the Sender of the collective actant: that is the role of 'tradition', which assigns to each their respective roles and competences. Thus the priest does not make the people competent, nor the people make the priest competent. Competence derives from the roles assigned by tradition and invested in the spatial configuration.

The priest also plays the role of 'spokesman' or delegated subject of an enunciative performance, on behalf of the whole collective actant in addressing an absent or invisible enunciatee, God. The collective nature of this performance is sanctioned by the 'Amen' uttered by those assembled in (9). Thus the respective *topoi* are also invested with this additional competence of 'being able to pray as a collectivity'.

2.1.4. *The Lectern*

By assuming his or her place at the lectern at the ritually designated moment, the reader is invested with the modal value of 'being-able-to-perform-the-ritual-act-of-reading', which is quite a different competence from that of following the reading in a mass-book. In relation to this same performance, the ministers and people are conjoined with their respective seats, thereby being modalized as 'hearers of the word'. The fact that the priest sits, rather than stands at his presidential seat means that his 'presidential' role, described above, is suspended but not negated, while he identifies with the rest of the collective actant (the congregation) in being modalized as a 'hearer'.

As 're-enunciator' of the scriptural text, the reader acts as delegated subject of the enunciation, acting on behalf of other delegated senders (the human authors of the Bible) and ultimately on behalf of God as original sender. In this way, an absent enunciator is able to communicate with the present enunciatee.

2.1.5. *The Altar*

The altar is a pole which, like the chair and the lectern, governs the whole *topos* of the main church, but which invests distinctive competencies in those who are physically conjoined with it and those who are only visually conjoined with it. In contrast to the chair and the lectern, however, the altar is a polar topos where a series of narrative performances transpire which have both cognitive and pragmatic dimensions. The pragmatic dimension consists of the collection and subsequent distribution of certain objects (bread and wine) which are transformed by being invested with specific modal and descriptive values as the result of the cognitive performance. The cognitive performance consists in the modalizing of the collective actant in terms of 'being-willing-to-participate' in the collective performance of sanctioning and petitioning God, in the performance of such manipulation and petition, in the sanctioning of the transformation of the value objects, and in manipulating the assembly to consume the value objects. For the pragmatic performance, some people from (9) become competent delegated subjects by entering (10). The priest is invested with the competence to sanction and manipulate God for the transformation of the value-objects by moving from his chair to the altar. The people in (9) first sanction this competence (opening dialogue) and then the performance itself ('Amen', 'Agnus Dei').

Thus the altar is first of all, like the chair, a pole or topos which invests those conjoined with it with the competence to address an absent or invisible enunciatee. Secondly, like the lectern, it is the topos in which the invisible subject of the enunciation communicates an object of value to the collective actant as enunciatee. This object of value invests the collective actant with the descriptive value of 'communion' or /unity/ both in terms of the internal relations of its members as parts to a whole, and in terms of the relationship of the visible subject to the invisible subject of the enunciation.

2.1.6. *The Organ*

The organ invests the subject who is physically conjoined with it with the pragmatic modal value of 'being able to make music' (not to be confused with the cognitive modal value of 'knowing how to make music'). As a pole in its own right, it invests the seats nearest to it with the competence to undertake specific musical performances in the course of the base program of the liturgy, either alone or in dialogue with the rest of the assembly. The organ also modalizes the assembly to undertake its own proper musical performances, either of singing or listening.

2.1.7. The *Dagkapel*

The weekday chapel is a configuration of two *topoi*, like the main church, but the topoi here are invested with a slightly different set of competences. For one thing, there is no organ in the congregational space

(5), so that the competence to play, to sing as a choir, and to sing as a congregation are not invested in the actants. Second, the different arrangement of the congregational space alters the mutual relationship between members of the collective actant and between them and the priest.

As to the first, the linear arrangement of the seats permits physical conjunction and prevents face-to-face interaction, thus the competence to be an assembly is aspectualized as 'weak'. Furthermore, the fact that the relationship to the priest is one of physical disjunction plus visual conjunction (face-to-face, but across the substantial barrier of the altar) accentuates the hypotactic nature of the relationship and weakens the collective category in which that relationship is contained in the main church. Indeed, the relationship is more polemical than contractual, since the topical arrangement invests the two topoi of (5) and (6) with non-interchangeable modal values. (There is, for example, no seat, so the priest does the reading and his 'presidential' competence is never neutralized as it is in the main church.) Thus the modal values associated with (9) are downgraded and those associated with (10) are accentuated.

2.1.8. *The Baptistry*

In complete contrast, the baptistry is a much more contractual setting. It is hexagonal and has a bench running around the walls. There is no special seat, nor is there a platform in the middle. However, the font serves as an anti-pole to the benches and thus sets up a possible opposition between those who sit near the wall and those who stand near the font. However loose, this arrangement nonetheless establishes a minimal 'modal structure of power'.

2.1.9. *The Devotional Areas*

Since the devotional areas, from the marian shrine to the memorials for the dead, are *topoi* for narrative programs with individual subjects performing them, it makes no sense to speak of them as being contractual or polemical in structure. Nonetheless, they are *topoi* which invest those who are spatially and temporally conjoined with them with the modal value of 'being able to do' the specific performance. Of course, all *topoi* require both spatial and temporal conjunction, but the importance of both criteria becomes apparent when the *topoi* concerned are only partially bounded or not bounded at all. To be able to pray the 'Stations of the Cross', for example, requires that person be close enough to be able to distinguish one 'station' from the next and spend a minimal amount of time at each station. Someone passing by cannot 'make the Stations', nor can someone who is located at such a distance as to be visually and physically disjoined.

2.2. Narrative Semantics

The *topoi* we have been examining are empty spaces waiting to become human places in being filled with actors. In these places, the actors assume different actantial roles and thus participate in the circulation of values. Yet one of the characteristic features, perhaps, of churches is the fact that the ultimate subject who is discoursivized as the enunciative partner of the collective actant (God) is not figurativized except indirectly in the *poles* with which the delegated subjects of the enunciation are conjoined: the chair, the lectern (cognitive communication) and the altar (pragmatic communication).

Conjunction with these poles and with their corresponding *topoi* in (9) and (10) invests the subjects with the appropriate modal values required by the delegated enunciator and the collective enunciatee. These are the modal values of 'being able to speak/act for God' and 'being able to address God', 'being able to listen to God' and 'being able to receive the gifts of God'. But these modal values at the level of the enunciation logically presuppose the constitution of the collective actant who is to be invested with such further modalizations: 'being able to do' presupposes a realized state of 'being able to be'.
Hence the specific performances of the narrative programs of Word and Sacrament have to be preceded by the constituting of the assembly in the opening rites, just as they will be followed by the dissolution of the collective actant.

Thus we have to distinguish:

    a. being able to be: competence to acquire the descriptive value of /collective being/;
    b. being able to do: competence to assume specific actantial roles within the collective actant;
    c. being able to be: competence to acquire the descriptive values which are the teleology of the narrative programs of (b).

At level (a) the descriptive values are those of /individual/ vs /collective/, for the transformation is from a roomful of individuals to an assembled people, a single moral person. This comes about through the conjunction of all parties with their respective poles and presupposes in turn, as we saw, the modal values of 'being able to institute the collective actant' and 'being able to be constituted as collective actant'.

At level (b) the values assumed by conjunction with the various *topoi* are modal values: being able to pray as a collectivity, being able to pray on behalf of the collectivity, being able to act as delegated enunciator, being able to listen to the word of God, being able to make music, and so on.

At level (c) the descriptive values are those for which the narrative programs of Word and Sacrament are undertaken. In the first case, the liturgy of the Word is intended to communicate a cognitive object which may often be modal (manipulation, know-how, sanction), but which is always descriptive because the communication always has a phatic dimension: the relationship between the enunciator and the enunciatee. (The same must also be said of the 'prayer' offered by the community to God.) In the second case, the communication of a descriptive object (the eucharist) may also be modalizing (as a source of actual grace), but is intended to transform not only the competence, but the being of the communicants, both in their relationship to God and to one another. Thus the transition is from /not knowing/ and /not being related/ to /knowing/ and /being related/: in both instances the relationship is a relationship to God and to the collective actant in whose midst and by whose performances the ultimate Sender is represented.

To these values associated with the objects in the narrative syntax we can compare the values we identified as the thematic trajectories. We identified six narrative trajectories which we can now set out together with their classematic values:

1. 'communal' vs 'quasi-communal celebrations'
   band 'public events' vs 'private devotions'.

2. 'community acts' vs 'ministerial acts'
   These can be reduced to the contraries /communal/ and /private/, with /ministerial/ and /quasi-communal/ as the subcontraries.

3. 'crowd' vs 'community', as 'virtual collective actant' vs 'realized collective actant'
   This can be formulated more abstractly as the opposition between /individual/ and /communal/.

4. 'tradition' vs 'modernity'
   which can be reduced to the semes /past/ vs /present/.

5. 'in the midst' vs 'beyond'.

6. 'this worldly' vs 'otherworldly'
   can be reduced to the semes /here/ vs /there/.

3. THE DEEP LEVEL

Is it possible, out of all the different thematic and classematic oppositions to find a single semantic opposition running through them all which would constitute the elementary structure of the signification?

At the discursive level we identified a basic opposition running through the whole building: 'in the midst' vs 'beyond'.
This seems to constitute a basic tension in the building. /in the midst/ gives rise to the human scale, the embedding, the minimalization of sacred or other-worldly isotopies, the general 'levelling out' of differences, the predominance of the collective over the individual or semi-public narrative programs. On the other hand, the /beyond/ generates the peculiar actantial roles (ministerial roles of 'priest' and 'reader' as filling the actantial role of a delegated subject who is not delegated by the assembly, for example), the presence of traditional sacramental sign-objects (font, altar, lectern), and the presence of iconic and scripted representations of the other-worldly community (saints, the dead).

However, even when reduced to the classematic opposition between /here/ and /there/ it does not prove comprehensive enough to include all the other themes. For this we must reduce it again by stripping it of its spatiality and rendering it as the simple opposition, /presence/ vs /absence/.

Set out on the semiotic square, together with the oppositions it generates, this gives the following constitutional model of the semantic micro-universe of the building:[3]

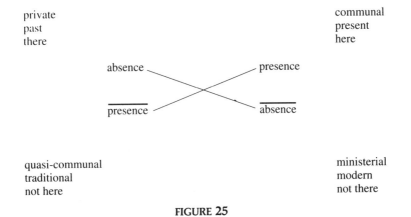

private
past
there

communal
present
here

absence — presence

presence — absence

quasi-communal
traditional
not here

ministerial
modern
not there

FIGURE 25

3. As for the meaning of the horizontal line over the words 'presence' and 'absence', expressing their negations, see page 59, footnote 9.

The tension in the building and in the performances it houses is revealed on the modal model of the elementary structures:

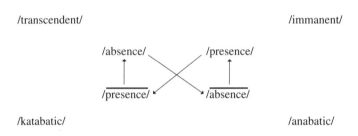

FIGURE 26

It is in the incessant negation and assertion of these oppositions that the identity of the church of SS. Peter and Paul is constituted. This not only corresponds to Claude Calame's claim that the fundamental syntax of mythical discourse consists of asserting both contrary terms of the discourse to be true (Calame in Greimas/Courtés 1986: 149); it also corresponds to the contraries figurativized in the pair of foundational figures to whom the building is dedicated: the apostles Peter and Paul.

4. THE PLANE OF THE EXPRESSION AND THE PLANE OF THE CONTENT

If we now compare the values we have identified as the elementary structure of the content with the values we identified on the plane of the expression, not everything on the plane of the expression seems to be equally pertinent. Nonetheless, some correlations can be identified:

absence	<u>presence</u>	<u>absence</u>	presence
<u>INDIV/SOCIAL</u> [4 & 7]	<u>INDIV/SOCIAL</u> [5-6 & 8]	INDIV/SOCIAL [10]	<u>INDIV/SOCIAL</u> [9]
peripheral not defined but defining linear	peripheral defined and defining linear or centred	central defined not defining centrifugal	central defined and defining centripetal

no nat. light	filtered light	direct light	direct light
[candle/spot]*	candle + spot	candle + spot	------
undefined	hexagon	hexagon	hexagon
	pentagon		
	rectangle		

FIGURE 27

*(7) has candles and spotlights; some of the poles in (4) have candles.

The problems lie with the categories of individual/social and individual/social. The baptistry (hexagonal, centered) falls under the first, as does the sanctuary (6: linear, pentagonal), whereas they are 'ministerial' spaces and should fall under the second.

On the other hand, it is also possible to make these other correlations of 'time' and 'focus':

absence	presence	absence	presence
INDIV/SOCIAL	INDIV/SOCIAL	INDIV/SOCIAL	INDIV/SOCIAL
past/present	past/present	past/present	past/present
there/here	there/here	there/here	there/here

FIGURE 28

C. CONCLUSION

The purpose of semiotic analysis, whether it be of written texts or of brick and concrete buildings, is not to offer the definitive 'reading', but to explore the structures of signification that make any reading possible. It does not resolve the 'conflict of interpretations' which Ricoeur has identified as characteristic of the humanities, but it should be able to demonstrate how well-founded such interpretations are. Yet, as this attempt to analyze the church of SS. Peter and Paul must surely have demonstrated, semiotic analysis itself, for all its methodological rigour, can only in the end offer a hypothetical construct of the structures of signification and always remains open to the possibility that a more perceptive or rigorous analysis may suggest another, better hypothesis. Thus, for semiotics, as for hermeneutics, the 'text' (in whatever medium) remains more than the sum of its interpretations.

Even so, a semiotic analysis of a building or a poem will always leave some loose ends, not only because of the deficiencies of the analysis, but also because of the deficiencies of the text itself. There is no such thing as a perfect poem or a perfect building, but only approximations to perfection in which not everything will be significant, and in which not everything that is significant will quite achieve the same transparency of form to content. This problem of 'loose ends' and ambiguities is clearly seen in the case of ordinary speech, which is rarely precise or eloquent, and which may prove quite incoherent when read back out of context. Nevertheless, people do succeed in communicating more or less adequately, and the same can be said of other more formal acts of human creativity, such as religious rites or public architecture. By attempting to account for how meaning-effects are produced, semiotics can also contribute to more sucessful communication. Semiotic analysis of church architecture will serve, it is hoped, to raise the level of awareness among both architects and church people of how buildings have a voice of their own and may 'speak' in ways not foreseen or intended by those who planned and erected them.

Bibliography

Augé, M. and Civil, R., Ermeneutica liturgica, in: S. Marsili *et al.* (ed.), *Anàmnesis. Introduzione storica-teologica alla Liturgia*, vol I: *La Liturgia, momento nella storia della salvezza*, Casale Monferrato 1974, 159-207

Berg, M. van den, *Samenwerkingsvormen in de bouw*, Deventer 1990

Bertrand, D., *L'espace et le sens*, Paris-Amsterdam 1985

Blaauw, S. de, Architecture and Liturgy in late Antiquity and the Middle Ages, in: *Archiv für Liturgiewissenschaft* 33 (1991) 1-34

Blijlevens, A. *et al.*, *Ruimte voor liturgie. Opstellen met betrekking tot de restauratie van de Sint Servaas in Maastricht*, Maastricht 1983

Calame, C. and Levy, A., Approches de l'espace, in: *Degrés. Revue de synthèse à l'orientation sémiologique* 11 (1983) no 35-36

Castex, J. and Pannerai, J., Structures de l'espace architectural, in: *Sémiotique de l'espace. Architecture, urbanisme, sortir de l'impasse*, Paris 1979, 61-93

Courtés, J., *Analyse sémiotique du discours. De l'énoncé à l'énonciation*, Paris 1991

Darrault, Y., L'espace de la thérapie, in: *Espace. Construction et signification. Sémiotique de l'architecture*, Paris 1984, 129-138

Escande, J., Les "patates" de Le Corbusier ou comment lire l'informel. Analyse d'un élément architectural du couvent Le Corbusier à L'Arbresle, in: *Sémiotique et Bible* 10 (1982) 33-39

Floch, J.M., La génération d'un espace commercial, in: *Actes Sémiotiques. Documents* 9 (1987) no 87, 5-29

Fontanille, J., *Les espaces subjectifs*, Paris 1989

Greimas, A.J., L'actualité du saussurisme, in: *Le français moderne* (1956) no 3

Greimas, A.J., *Sémantique structurale*, Paris 1966, republication Paris 1986 (Engl. transl. by D. McDowell, R. Schleiffer and A. Velie, *Structural Semantics. An Attempt at a Method*, Lincoln, Nebr.1983)

Greimas, A.J., *Du sens. Essais sémiotiques*, Paris 1970 (Engl. transl. by P. Perron and F. Collins, *On Meaning. Selected Writings in Semiotic Theory by A.J. Greimas*, Minneapolis 1987)

Greimas, A.J. (ed.), *Essais de sémiotique poétique*, Paris 1972

Greimas, A.J., *Sémiotique et sciences sociales*, Paris 1976 (a) (Engl. transl. by P. Perron and F. Collins, *The Social Sciences. A Semiotic View*, Minneapolis (in preparation))

Greimas, A.J., Pour une sémiotique topologique, in: *Sémiotique de l'espace. Architecture, urbanisme, sortir de l'impasse*, Paris 1979, 11-43 (included in: A.J. Greimas, *Sémiotique et sciences sociales*, Paris 1976 (a))

Greimas, A.J., *Maupassant. La sémiotique du texte*, Paris 1976 (b) (Engl. transl. by P. Perron, *Maupassant. The Semiotics of Text. Practical Exercises*, Amsterdam 1988)

Greimas, A.J. and Courtés, J., *Sémiotique. Dictionnaire raisonné de la théorie du langage*, vol. I, Paris 1979 (Engl. transl. by L. Christ *et al.*, *Semiotics and Language. An Analytical Dictionary*, Bloomington, Ind. 1982)

Greimas, A.J., *Du sens II. Essais sémiotiques*, Paris 1983

Greimas, A.J., Sémiotique figurative et sémiotique plastique, in: *Actes Sémiotiques. Documents* 6 (1984) no 60

Greimas, A.J., *Des dieux et des hommes. Etudes de mythologie lithuanienne*, Paris 1985 (Engl. transl. by M. Newman, *On Gods and Men*, Bloomington, Ind. (in preparation))

Greimas, A.J. and Courtés, J., *Sémiotique. Dictionnaire raisonné de la théorie du langage*, vol. 2, Paris 1986

Greimas, A.J., *De l'imperfection*, Périgueux 1987 (Engl. transl. by T. Keane, *On Imperfection*, Amsterdam (in preparation))

Greimas, A.J. and Fontanille, J., *Des états de choses aux états d'âmes. Essais de sémiotique des passions*, Paris 1990 (Engl. transl. by P. Perron and F. Collins, *Semiotics of passion. From states of affairs to states of feeling*, Minneapolis 1992; with bibliographical references)

Hammad, M., Arango, S., Kuyper, E. de, Poppe, E., L'espace du séminaire, in: *Communications* 27 (1977) 28-54

Hammad, M., Définition syntaxique du topos, in: *Actes Sémiotiques. Le Bulletin* 3 (1979) no 10, 25-27 (a)

Hammad, M., Espaces didactiques: analyse et conception, in: *Actes Sémiotiques. Le Bulletin* 2 (1979) no 7, 30-32 (b)

Hammad, M., L'espace comme sémiotique syncrétique, in: *Actes Sémiotiques. Le Bulletin* 6 (1983), no 27, 26-30

Hammad, M., Rituels sacrés/rituels profanes. Usages signifiants de l'espace, in: *Espace. Construction et signification. Sémiotique de l'architecture*, Paris 1984, 215-240

Hammad, M., Primauté heuristique du contenu, in: H. Parret and H. G. Ruprecht (ed.), *Exigences et perspectives de la sémiotique. Recueil d' hommages pour Algirdas Julien Greimas*, vol. I, Amsterdam 1985, 229-240

Hammad, M., L'architecture du thé, in: *Actes Sémiotiques. Documents* 9 (1987) no 84-85, 1-50

Hammad, M., La privatisation de l'espace, in: *Nouveaux Actes Sémiotiques* 1 (1989) no 4 and 5

Kuyper, E. de, Le Perçu et le Nommé van Christian Metz. Een commentariërende lectuur, in: *Versus* 5 (1986) no 3, 115-126

Levy, A., *Sémiotique de l'espace: architecture classique sacrée* (Thèse de 3e cycle, dir. A.J. Greimas, EHSS), Paris 1979 (polycopiée)

Levy, A., Les différents niveaux de signification dans la construction de l'espace architectural, in: *Degrés. Revue de synthèse à orientation sémiologique* 11 (1983) no 35-36, i, 1-18

Lukken, G., Het binnengaan in de kerk in de nieuwe Romeinse huwelijksliturgie: een semiotische analyse, in: *Jaarboek voor Liturgie-onderzoek* 1 (1985) 69-89

Lukken, G., Een bidprentje, in: SEMANET (ed. G. Lukken), *Semiotiek en christelijke uitingsvormen. De semiotiek van A.J. Greimas en de Parijse school toegepast op bijbel en liturgie*, Hilversum 1987 (a)

Lukken, G., Semiotische analyse van de huwelijkssluiting in het post-tridentijnse Rituale Romanum, in: *Jaarboek voor Liturgie-onderzoek* 3 (1987) 41-85 (b)

Lukken, G., De semiotiek van de kerkruimte als semiotiek van het visuele, in: *Jaarboek voor Liturgie-onderzoek* 5 (1989) 275-299 (a)

Lukken, G., Die architektonischen Dimensionen des Rituals, in: *Liturgisches Jahrbuch* 39 (1989) 19-36 (b) (French transl.: Les dimensions architectoniques du rituel, in: *Sémiotique et Bible* 16 (1991) no 61, 5-21)

Lukken, G., Studieweek SEMANET-CADIR over semiotiek en christelijke uitingsvormen, in: *Jaarboek voor Liturgie-onderzoek* 1989, 134 and *Tijdschrift voor Theologie* 29 (1989) 391-392 (c)

Lukken, G., Les transformations du rôle du peuple: la contribution de la sémiotique à l'histoire de la liturgie, in: C. Caspers and M. Schneiders (ed.), *Omnes Circumadstantes. Contributions towards a history of the role of the people in the liturgy*, Kampen 1990, 15-30

Marsili, S. *et al.* (ed.), *Anàmnesis. Introduzione storico-teologica alla Liturgia*, 5 vols., Casale Monferrato 1979 ff.

Martimort, A.G. (ed.), *L'église en prière. Introduction à la liturgie*, Edition nouvelle, 4 vols., Paris 1983-1984

Metz, C., De onpersoonlijke enunciatie of de lokatie van de film. In de marge van recente studies naar de enunciatie in de cinema, in: *Versus* 7 (1988) no 3, 54-82. (or. title: L'énonciation impersonelle, ou le site du film. En marge de traveaux récents sur l'énonciation du cinéma, in: *Vertigo* 1 (1987) 13-35)

Muck, M., *Stadt- Wohn und Kirchenraum. Zur Strukturierung ihrer Beziehungen*, paper meeting AKL, September 1988, 5

Panier, L., Lecture sémiotique et projet théologique, in: *Recherches de Science Religieuse* 78 (1990) 199-220

Panier, L., Over figuren in het discours. Enkele overwegingen over de discursieve semiotiek, in: P. Beentjes, J. Maas and T. Wever (ed.), 'Gelukkig de mens'. Opstellen over psalmen, exegese en semiotiek aangeboden aan Nico Tromp, Kampen 1991, 182-192

Pavis, P., Problèmes de sémiotique théâtrale, Montréal 1976

Renier, A., Nature et lecture de l'espace architectural, in: Notes méthodologiques en architecture, 3-4, Institut de l'Environnement, Paris 1974 (Also in: Sémiotique de l'espace, D.G.R.S.T., Paris 1973 and in: Sémiotique de l'espace. Architecture, urbanisme, sortie de l'impasse, Paris 1979, 45-59)

Renier, A., L'école et l'architecture, in: Actes Sémiotiques. Le Bulletin 2 (1979) no 7, 27-29 (a)

Renier, A., Pour une sémiotique architecturale, in: Actes Sémiotiques. Le Bulletin 2 (1979) no 10, 3-6 (b)

Renier, A., Review of A. Levy, Sémiotique de l'espace: architecture classique sacrée, thèse de 3e cycle, E.H.E.S.S., 1979, in: Actes Sémiotiques. Le Bulletin 3 (1979) no 11, 45-51 (c)

Renier, A., Espace, représentation et sémiotique de l'architecture, in: A. Renier et al., Espace et Représentation, Paris 1982, 5-33

Renier, A., Domaines actuels de la recherche sémiotique. Architecture et sémiotique. Contribution de la sémiotique à la conception architecturale, in: Sémiotique et Bible 8 (1983) no 32, 12-18

Renier, A., Introduction au colloque, in: Espace. Construction et signification. Sémiotique de l'architecture, Paris 1984, 11-21

Renier, A., L'acquisition pragmatique des concepts sémiotiques relatifs à l'espace par les architectes, in: H. Parret and H.G. Ruprecht (ed.), Exigences et perspectives de la sémiotique. Recueil d'hommages pour Algirdas Julien Greimas, vol. II, Amsterdam 1985, 631-638

Renier, A., L'apport de la sémiotique à la conception architecturale, in: M. Arrivé and J.C. Coquet (ed.), Sémiotique en jeu. A partir et autour de l'oeuvre d' A.J. Greimas, Paris-Amsterdam 1987, 157-174

Rooy, M. van and Roodnat, B., De Stopera. Een Amsterdamse geschiedenis, Amsterdam – Brussel 1986

Schiwy, G. et al., Zeichen im Gottesdienst, München 1976

SEMANET (ed. G. Lukken), Semiotiek en christelijke uitingsvormen. De semiotiek van A.J. Greimas en de Parijse school toegepast op bijbel en liturgie, Hilversum 1987

Sémiotique de l'architecture, in: Actes Sémiotiques. Le Bulletin 2 (1979) no 10, 1-59

Semprini, A., Métro, réseau, ville. Essai de sémiotique topologique, in: Nouveaux Actes Sémiotiques 2 (1990) no 8

Senn, F., Eucharistic Prayers. An Ecumenical Study of their Development and Structure, New York 1987

Sequeira, R., Gottesdienst als menschliche Ausdruckshandlung, in: H.B. Meyer *et al.* (ed.), *Gottesdienst der Kirche. Handbuch der Liturgiewissenschaft*, vol. III: Gestalt der Gottesdienst, Regensburg 1987, (a)

Sequeira, R., Liturgy and Dance: on the Need for an adequate Terminology, in: *Gratias Agamus. An ecumenical collection of essays on the Liturgy and its implications on the occasion of the twenty fifth anniversary of Studia Liturgica (1962-1987)*, edited by W. Vos in cooperation with G. Wainwright, Liturgical Ecumenical Center Trust, Rotterdam 1987, 157-165 (= Studia Liturgica 17 (1987) 157-165) (b)

Simons, J., De enunciatie van de film, in: *Versus* 7 (1988) no 3, 89 ff.

Thürlemann, F., *Paul Klee. Analyse sémiotique de trois peintures*, Lausanne 1982

Zilberberg, C., Eléments pour une description de l'espace, in: *Espace. Construction et signification. Sémiotique de l'architecture*, Paris 1984, 47-61

Periodicals:

Actes Sémiotiques: 1. *Le Bulletin* 2. *Documents*

Since 1989: *Nouveaux Actes Sémiotiques*

Appendix Some data of the Church of SS. Peter and Paul, Tilburg

The Church of SS. Peter and Paul in Tilburg was built in the years 1968-1969. Its architect was Ir. H. Lelieveldt (1928), architectenbureau J.A. Lelieveldt, Rotterdam, its contractor the firm P.H. Meerendonk. The church was consecrated November 29, 1969. Luc van Hoek from Goirle (The Netherlands), designed the small shrine on the front side of the altar, scultress Edith Peres-Lethmate from Koblenz (Switzerland) made the crucifix. The statue of St. Joseph in the day-church is by the sculptor Hans Claesen from Tilburg. The Lady Chapel contains a 17th century wood carved statue of the Virgin Mary. Its windows and the window of the baptistery are by Marius de Leeuw from Vught (The Netherlands). The costs of the building, including ground, inventory, car park, **pastorie**, pavement and crops, amounted to a total of f.820.000.

cross section

longitudinal section

| 0 | 5 | 10 meter |

S.S. Petrus & Paulus - Tilburg - Netherlands

ir. h. h. j. lelieveldt b.i. b.n.a.   postbus 4025   3006 AA rotterdam